FAMILY STORM

Surviving the Turbulence

BEATRICE NDUDIM GOLDSON-NWALOZIE

FAMILY STORM

Surviving the Turbulence

BEATRICE NDUDIM GOLDSON-NWALOZIE

ARPress
ILLUMINATING IDEAS
EMPOWERING VOICES

ARPress
45 Dan Road Suite 15
Canton MA 02021
 Hotline: 1(888) 821-0229
 Fax: 1(508) 545-7580

Ordering Information:
Quantity sales. Special discounts are available on quantity purchases by corporations, associations, and others. For details, contact the publisher at the address above.

Printed in the United States of America.

ISBN-13:   Softcover   979-8-89676-379-6
           eBook   979-8-89676-380-2

Library of Congress Control Number: 2025916165

TABLE OF CONTENTS

DEDICATION

"FAMILY STORM" is dedicated to families dealing with divorce and marital challenges, especially those facing complex transitions with children. The book acknowledges the emotional difficulties and offers understanding during these times. It provides guidance and support for families experiencing divorce and marital disruption.

ACKNOWLEDGEMENT

I am deeply grateful to Professor Pai Obanya, former UNESCO Director in Dakar, Senegal, for his steadfast support and encouragement throughout the writing of this book.

I wish to express my sincere appreciation to my esteemed friends and colleagues for their valuable guidance and support throughout the development of this book: Mrs. Obiageri Akajelu of the Ministry of Foreign Affairs, Nigeria, and Mrs. Ngozi Obinani, former Deputy Director, Federal Ministry of Education, Abuja.

Dr. Mrs. Patience Ozor, Alvan Ikoku College of Education, Owerri, Imo State. Dr. Mrs. Bridget Ikegwuru, Federal Ministry of Education, (FME), Abuja.

Mrs. Constance M. Kalu Nwoke, Chief Scientific Officer, State Ministry of Health, Umuahia, Abia State.

Barr. Mrs. Pearl Ehiringa, Imo State University, Owerri.

I would like to express my gratitude to Mrs. Claris Ujam, Deputy Director at the Federal Ministry of Education, Abuja, Prof. Mrs. Chidi Nwosu from Imo State University, Owerri, Nigeria.

Mr. & Mrs. Raymond Okoroji of MTA, New York. I truly appreciate your invaluable efforts and excellent advice. Thank you.

I am grateful to my beautiful, handsome, and wonderful children—Chichi (Florida), Akachi (California), and Chubby (Chicago)—through whom God made me a joyful mother of three.

I am grateful for their unwavering support throughout the writing of this book. Thank you for sharing my journey. May you all be blessed.

I also dedicate this book to my two fantastic grandchildren, Oscar Kelechi, A and William Chinedu, A.(Tampa, Florida).

This page cannot be completed without my special thanks to the UNESCO Library, Brenda, Dakar, Senegal for providing me with most of the books used and the Public Library, Eastchester, E. Gun Hill Road, Bronx, New York, for assisting me with the very important books that were relevant and useful to everyone. My heartfelt thanks.

Next, I wish to acknowledge my mother, Mrs. Dorah Nwanyinnaya Goldson, for bringing me into this world and raising me to be a strong, courageous, cheerful, beautiful (Nwaenyerenma, which means 'a child endowed with beauty': as she fondly called me), hardworking, respectful, industrious, educated, and God-fearing young woman.

My mother, Mrs. Dorah Nwanyinnaya Goldson, was a beautiful, hardworking, rich business woman, a principled woman with character and integrity, wisdom and discernment, emotional strength, compassion and empathy, self-respect and boundaries, purpose and drive, accountability—she owns her decisions, grace under pressure, capacity to nurture growth, faith and moral anchor, and her leadership style is impeccable.

She unfortunately died in July 2004. May her gentle soul continue to rest in PEACE. Amen.

I also appreciate my spiritual leaders Venerable Reverend David Nwanekpe and Reverend Clifford Erondu the Priests in my church, 'Anglican Church of the Holy Spirit', Bronx, New York for playing various Godly roles in my life.

I want to acknowledge and appreciate the Almighty, All-sufficient God who gave me the grace, strength, knowledge, wisdom, exciting, great, and healthy life to start and complete this work at the appropriate time. All glory, honor, power, dominion, excellence, majesty, and adoration be ascribed unto Him alone. Amen.

God the Father, Son, and the Holy Spirit, my protective and dependable Yahweh, the solid rock on which I stand, my fortress, refuge and defender who because of Him I am able to start this wonderful book and conclude with grace, good health, wisdom, favor and many other good things. I salute you, the Most High God, my Able, Awesome Father. Nmanma.

PREFACE

Originally titled "Family Drama," this book began in 1999 in Dakar, Senegal, inspired by a difficult family experience. Colleagues recommended that I share my experience to support others encountering comparable challenges.

I'm rebranding my book, "Family Storm: Surviving the Turbulence," which began in 2025 in New York. My goal is to share its insights with today's generation, who I feel need them now more than ever.

The themes explored in *Family Storm: Surviving the Turbulence* are particularly timely, given that many families today encounter emotional, social, and moral issues that can threaten their stability.

This rebranding is intended to help modern readers see that family challenges are inevitable, but with faith, love, and resilience, families can overcome difficulties and grow stronger.

I'm thankful it's finally here.

ENDORSEMENT OF THE BOOK "FAMILY STORM", FOR BEATRICE GOLDSON-NWALOZIE BY DR. PASTOR NGOZI OBINANI

FAMILY STORM is a very timely book, loaded with vital insights garnered from research, observation, and experience by the author, Beatrice Goldson-Nwalozie, a two-time writer of published books. Timely and topical, this book delved into the issue of a key institution, divinely created by God Almighty, to be the founding cell for, and essential nucleus of the human society, for purposes that include companionship; procreation to preserve and replenish human life on earth; mutual help with the productive work that God wisely provided in the "garden"; partnership in enjoying the benefits arising from work done in dignity and accountability; exercising the dominion that the Creator God gave man over His entire creation.

A professionally trained Teacher, Guidance Counselor, and Substance Use Specialist, with wide practice in these three areas of specialization acquired and practiced within two countries—Nigeria and USA. Goldson-Nwalozie is in her element as teacher, counselor, and specialist in substance abuse, to delve into the relational issue of marriage. She, herself, is also one who has experienced marriage and family life, as wife, mother and grandmother, based on biblical principles; her presentations in this book on marriage issues are, therefore, authentic.

Concerning inclusion of her specialty on substance abuse, as an important content of this endorsement, are not some of the problems that whip up storms in marriage caused by abuse of one substance or another? The range of marital abuse engaged in, out of selfish and self-centered considerations and ego-tripping behavior patterns that lead to emotional storms arising from mood-altering of one's consciousness and memory that inhibit or violate the abuser's acknowledgement, respect, and honoring the Divine Author of Marriage, and commitment to his or her marriage vows, is very startling in its negative impact marriage, and on society at large! Do we not have the Marriage Manufacturer's Manual in the Bible that He gave wisdom and divine inspiration to holy, human writers to pen down for guiding would-be operators of marriage, to keep it holy and undefiled, even as the Author meant this institution to be?

Goldson-Nwalozie teaching talents include astutely breaking down, and pulling out biblical principles, to equip readers, and influence positive change in behavior, that can calm storms, including marital ones. This is the goal of the teaching-learning enterprise; this is the same goal that she pursued in FAMILY STORM, as is reflected in its sub-title, Surviving the Turbulence.

I have known and observed, at close quarters, the progressive and consistent growth of Beatrice, from the year 2004 when she joined the Federal Ministry of Education, headquarters in Abuja when she was a Senior Cadre Officer. I was supervising her handling of her schedule on Bilateral Agreement with every other country in the field of education and multilateral agreement relations in international education, I took notice of and developed deepening interest in Beatrice Goldson-Nwalozie manifestation of quick understanding of, and intelligent, diligent and reliable handling of her assigned responsibilities. I am also one of her mentors in spiritual ministry. Since I reconnected with her in New York, I have observed that her level of personality and performance excellence has not abetted, but rather, has been progressively rising. She has, added to her credentials and rising profile through continuing formal education and its attendant research imperatives, and has grown so much in professional status over the years. Beatrice is doing so well as a Substance Use Specialist in her organization. She has added more feathers to her qualification and training as a smart, hardworking woman. Here in the USA.

Her book, FAMILY STORM: with the subtitle 'Surviving the Turbulence' bears loaded evidence of her mark as teacher, researcher, counselor, and professional adviser, with all these strands astutely woven together into her gifts and talents as a twice-published author and giver of problem-solving guidelines for surviving marriage and family storms. This is a non-fictional work, this book is a big chunk of life, to borrow and modify Honoré Balzac's concept of novels as "A slice of Life".

Based on my personal knowledge of the capabilities of the author given above, I highly recommend Goldson-Nwalozie book 'FAMILY STORM: Surviving the Turbulence' to readers interested in, affected by, and/or burdened with finding keys for success in marriage as originally designed by its Divine Author, or with finding solutions to existing marital storms; this book is both preventive and curative in its impact, and has great potential for global applicability and universal impact.

A vibrant, joyful, and close-knit family

INTRODUCTION

FAMILY STRUCTURE

Family life nurtures growth and well-being, especially for children, through love, respect, equality, and strong inter-generational ties. Sociologically, families serve as centers for reproduction, child-rearing, emotional support, and socialization. Traditionally, they also function as economic units where household members work together in home-based or agricultural activities.

Households or family members depend on and participate in these functions to differing extents throughout their lives. Simultaneously, the roles fulfilled by individual household members are frequently shaped by specific family characteristics—such as size, type, or structure—which in turn influence the relationships and responsibilities among members.

Families are typically classified as nuclear or extended. A nuclear family includes a married couple and their unmarried children, or a single parent with unmarried children. An extended family adds other relatives or, occasionally, unrelated individuals. Extended families can be vertical, such as three generations living together, or horizontal, like joint families with multiple brothers, their wives, and children—a pattern seen in traditional Hindu society in India (Adams, 1986).

We are created to love and be loved, and there is no greater opportunity for this love than in marriage. We are called to become one with another so that we can touch each other's deepest needs: the need for security—knowing that we are loved—and the need for significance—knowing that we are valued. So why is marriage disintegrating? Lack of love, communication, migration.

To be successful in marriage, you must be solid, responsible, and whole. That means you must love yourself, delight in the unique creation of you, and appreciate the unique creation reflected in others. You must be able to love yourself before you can love anyone else, study yourself, and your purpose in life—yet marriage will not tolerate selfishness. We all desperately long for a happy relationship. We were born into relationships, helpless and vulnerable, and had it not been relationships, we would have perished. Not much has changed except that we can physically survive.

Couples strive to build stable homes for their families, but family challenges often stem from broader economic, social, and demographic shifts. Most parents require support at crucial times, especially those facing vulnerabilities such as single-parenthood, financial hardship, or immigration. This need extends to communities and society.

The aim of social support is not to take away parental functions or to make families passive recipients of social care. Having children creates responsibility and will normally motivate parents to carry out their biological, psychological, economical, and educational functions: to impart care and protection; often love and healthy family relationships; provide shelter and material welfare; promote play and learning. Societies will do well, however, to support responsible attitudes to parenthood by educating adolescents and young adults in parenting skills and providing support systems for parents in their child-rearing tasks.

The 1994 International Year of the Family encourages us to consider the family as the "smallest democracy at the heart of society." One common issue is the widespread phenomenon of absent fathers. This lack of involvement often stems from deep-rooted cultural beliefs and gender stereotypes, though sometimes it's due to external reasons like work-related migration. Even under ideal conditions, fathers frequently spend limited time with their children. Studies show that this can leave mothers overwhelmed by responsibilities and boys negatively affected by the absence of their fathers. Additionally, when fathers do not provide support, many female-led households face economic challenges.

For families left behind by migrant members, adjustments must be made not only for the absence—whether temporary or permanent—but also for the new money, goods, ideas, attitudes, and behaviors brought back by those who moved away. How families adapt depends on which members migrate, how long they are gone, and the cultural context of their home environment.

The nuclear family tends to be more economically sustainable than extended family groups, which have become less common in urban areas. Patterns of rural-to-urban migration often reinforce this trend. Census data indicates, for example, that approximately 80% of migrants to Indian cities reside in nuclear families rather than within traditional joint family systems. According to the 1992 Marriage and Recession annual report by the UK Marriage Guidance Group, factors such as unemployment, redundancy, home repossessions, and increasing debts can significantly disrupt and adversely impact family life.

African families face significant challenges. During the 1990s, average per-capita income dropped by 25%, and between 1979 and 1985, the number of Africans living below the poverty line increased by almost two-thirds. While per-capita incomes have also fallen in Latin America and parts of Asia—sometimes offsetting progress seen in places like China—in Africa, environmental decline, population growth, and food insecurity have together weakened families' ability to cope, a situation made worse by national debt and global recession.

Many important events take place in the home. It is here that family members receive shelter and sustenance. Home is possibly the most important place in all our lives; it is where we belong and feel secure. Some family members can never leave home or establish an independent life. This may be due to illness or disability; it may be due to infirmity in old age.

When there is no broader support available, families act as a haven for individuals who cannot look after themselves. In fact, the family serves as the world's primary welfare institution. Just as a mother's body first protects her developing child, the family surrounds its members with care—a true "haven in a heartless world." In most cultures, mothers typically tend to infants; spending so much time together helps mothers and children form strong emotional bonds and get to know each other deeply.

Family relationships serve as a significant source of well-being and identity for individuals. Within families, emotional dynamics such as love, affection, anger, and aggression are commonly expressed. The expression of emotion is essential to children's development and is often fostered through play. Typically, family members experience their closest interactions during leisure activities. Furthermore, the provision of recreational opportunities is recognized as an important role of the family unit.

Evidence clearly shows that a child who is neglected physically, mentally, or emotionally will suffer disadvantages which may last a lifetime. The family is still regarded as the best environment for a young child's nurture and upbringing, even in disadvantaged circumstances. In a troubled family, the reverse is the case, but overall, parents try to avoid divided families. The thought of losing custody or worst still contact with the child is phobic. More so, vulnerable families—single-parent families, families without shelter or income, immigrant families, destabilized families, or families with special needs, need the support of the extended family, the community, and society at large.

NAVIGATING MARITAL STORMS WITH GOD

Navigating Life's Tempests Together Under Divine Guidance

Introduction

Marriage, in its essence, is a journey—an odyssey that two souls embark upon, promising to weather both sunshine and storm, calm and chaos. When the winds of life rise and the waves threaten to capsize the fragile vessel of togetherness, the image of marriage as a boat in the storm emerges with poignant clarity. Yet, for those who hold steadfast in faith, there is a third presence aboard: God, the divine helmsman, who not only steadies the trembling craft but also navigates it toward tranquil harbors. This essay explores the profound metaphor of marriage as a vessel tossed upon stormy seas, with God as the guiding force. It examines the symbolism, the challenges inherent in matrimonial union, and the transformative power of inviting the Divine into the center of the marital journey.

The Marriage Boat: Setting Sail Together

Marriage is like setting off in a boat on unfamiliar waters. The wedding marks the hopeful start as two people with different backgrounds begin their journey together. While there will be easy, joyful moments, challenges are inevitable for every couple.

The Inevitability of Storms

No marriage is immune to the tempests that life, in its unpredictability, inevitably brings. Storms may take the form of financial hardship, illness, betrayal, misunderstandings, grief, or the slow erosion of connection through daily stresses and unspoken hurt. Sometimes, the storm is external—a crisis that shakes the very foundations of family and home. Other times, the storm brews within, as hearts drift apart or conflicts ignite. In these moments, the boat is tested. The winds howl, and the oars splinter. Water pours over the sides, threatening to swamp carefully laid plans and dreams. Spouses may feel isolated, unable to hear one another above the roar of the gale, clinging to opposite ends of the boat, gripped by fear or anger. The temptation to abandon ships can be overwhelming.

God as the Divine Helmsman. And yet, in the chaos, there is an invitation to remember that the boat need not be steered by human hands alone. The presence of God in marriage is like an anchor during the storm and a compass in the fog. For those who seek Him, God is both a strong hand upon the tiller and the voice that whispers, "Peace, be still." Inviting God into the marriage boat does not mean that storms will cease. Rather, it means that there is a source of strength and wisdom greater than either spouse possesses alone. God's love, infinite and unconditional, becomes the standard against which all actions and words are measured. In the darkest moments, faith becomes a lantern illuminating the way forward.

Trusting in Divine Guidance

Trust is the currency of both marriage and faith. Just as spouses must learn to trust one another, so must they learn to trust that God is present, active, and faithful, even when all seems lost.

Prayers become lifelines, drawing the couple together and upward. Scripture becomes a map, offering both direction and hope.

When the waves crash and vision is lost, it is God who sees beyond the horizon. When exhaustion threatens to overwhelm, it is God who promises rest. When anger flares or words wound, it is God who teaches forgiveness and gentle speech. The storm does not define the voyage, but how the couple chooses to sail through it—with or without God—shapes the outcome.

Communication: The Oars That Propel the Boat

Even with God as a guide, the couple must work in tandem, rowing together rather than against one another. Communication is the oar that propels the boat; its absence leaves the vessel adrift. In the fury of the storm, clear and compassionate communication becomes vital.

God's presence inspires humility—the willingness to listen, to apologize, to seek understanding rather than victory. Praying together, even when words are hard to find, builds unity and reminds spouses that they are not adversaries, but partners joined by covenant.

Resilience Born of Faith

Storms, for all their violence, are not without purpose. They test and reveal character, forging resilience and deepening love. Couples who weather storms with God at the center emerge not unscathed, but transformed—more attuned to one another, more grateful for moments of calm, more trusting in God's sustaining power.

Faith does not eliminate pain, but it offers hope. It reminds the couple that the boat is not theirs alone to pilot, and that even when the night is at its blackest, the dawn will come. God's promises are the stars by which they can steer, reliable and luminous.

Practical Ways to Keep God at the Center

- Pray Together Daily: Set aside time to thank God for blessings, confess struggles, and ask for guidance.

- Study Scripture as a Couple: Let God's word be a foundation and source of discussion, comfort, and direction.
- Attend Fellowship: Engage with a community of faith where you can both give and receive support in times of need.
- Serve Together: Find ways to bless others as a team, strengthening your bond and shifting focus from personal storms to shared mission.
- Forgive Quickly: Embrace the mercy that God extends to you, and extend it to each other, refusing to let bitterness take root.

When the Storm Subsides

No storm lasts forever. When the tempest calms and sunlight returns, the boat may bear the scars of the ordeal, but it remains afloat—perhaps even more seaworthy than before. The couple, having clung not only to each other than God, discovers a new depth of love, gratitude, and awe. With hands clasped and hearts aligned, they can look back and say, "By God's grace, we have come through."

Conclusion

Marriage isn't a guarantee of constant peace, but rather an agreement to face life's challenges side by side. Difficult times will arise and sometimes feel overwhelming, yet with faith, humility, love, and trust in God, couples persevere. Even when trouble mounts and the winds grow fierce, they stay strong, comforted by knowing they're never truly alone on their journey.

Marriage serves as a vessel navigating the journey of life, with storms symbolizing challenges, while God continually leads, supports, and ultimately brings travelers safely home.

SURVIVING THE STORM: NAVIGATING TURBULENCE WITH KIDS AFTER SEPARATION AND DIVORCE

Resilience, Healing, and Hope for Families in Transition

Separation and divorce bring forth a tempest that blows through every corner of a family's life, uprooting routines, reconfiguring relationships, and demanding resilience from both parents and children. When the winds of change come howling, it can be difficult to see beyond the immediate turmoil. Yet, amid the turbulence, there exists a path toward healing, adjustment, and a new kind of harmony.

Understanding the Impact on Children

The emotional landscape for children in the wake of separation or divorce is complex and often tumultuous. Each child experiences this life-altering event through their own lens—shaped by age, temperament, and the nature of the family's transition.

- Emotional Responses: Children may feel sadness, anger, confusion, or even guilt. It's not uncommon for them to fear abandonment or worry that they are to blame for the changes at home.
- Behavioral Changes: Some may become withdrawn, while others act out. Academic performance can suffer, sleep patterns may change, and anxieties about the future might surface.
- Developmental Considerations: Younger children might struggle to understand the permanence of divorce; adolescents could feel pressure to choose sides or take on adult responsibilities.
- Recognizing these responses is the first step in helping children weather the turmoil. Compassionate listening and gentle reassurance lay the groundwork for stability.

The Parent's Role: Anchoring Amid Chaos

During upheaval, children rely on caregivers for guidance. Even amid their own struggles, parents can provide stability for the family.

- Modeling Emotional Regulation: Demonstrating healthy ways to process anger, sadness, and stress helps children develop resilience.
- Consistency and Routine: Predictable schedules provide a sense of security. Familiar rituals—bedtime stories, weekend outings, family meals—become lifelines amidst chaos.
- Clear Communication: Use simple, honest language to explain changes. Avoid blame or negative talk about the other parent.
- Validation and Support: Let children know that their feelings are valid. Encourage expression through words, art, play, or writing.

Creating Two Loving Homes

Separation doesn't mean the end of family, but rather its transformation. Children thrive when both homes are nurturing, respectful, and welcoming.

Collaborative Co-Parenting

Working together, even after the relationship ends, is perhaps the greatest gift parents can give their children.

- Respectful Communication: Keep exchanges focused on the child's needs, not unresolved adult conflicts.
- Shared Values: Agree on key rules and expectations across households—bedtimes, homework, screen time—to foster consistency.
- Flexibility and Compromise: Life will require adjustments; approach them as a team, keeping the child's well-being at the center.

When Co-Parenting Isn't Possible

In cases where communication is strained or unsafe, parallel parenting may be necessary. This approach minimizes direct interaction and sets clear boundaries, prioritizing children's safety and stability.

Supporting Children Through Transition

Honest Conversations

Children benefit from age-appropriate, truthful explanations about what is happening. Assure them that both parents' love is unwavering and emphasize that separation is a decision between adults—not a consequence of anything the child did.

Encouraging Expression

Invite children to share their feelings in whatever way they feel comfortable. Listen deeply, resist the urge to fix, and affirm their emotions.

Maintaining Connections

Help children maintain relationships with extended family, friends, and trusted adults. Social support can buffer stress and provide outlets for joy.

Preserving Traditions and Creating New Ones

Keep favorite family traditions alive but also invent new rituals that mark this chapter with hope and possibility. Whether it's a monthly movie night, a shared journal, or a simple walk in the park, these moments become anchors in the new normal.

Managing Your Own Turbulence

As a parent, tending to your own wounds is not a luxury, it's a necessity. The journey through separation and divorce is physically and emotionally taxing, and self-care is critical for showing up as your best self for your children.

- Seek Support: Therapy, support groups, and trusted friends can help process grief and offer perspective.
- Set Boundaries: Protect your mental space from unnecessary conflict. Prioritize your well-being.
- Allow Yourself to Heal: Forgive yourself for mistakes, let go of regret, and embrace new possibilities.

When Professional Help Is Needed

Sometimes, the turbulence is too great to navigate alone. Watch for signs that children need additional support:

- Persistent sadness or anxiety
- Withdrawal from friends or activities
- Significant changes in eating or sleeping
- Decline in school performance
- Talk of self-harm or hopelessness

If these arise, seek guidance from a counselor, pediatrician, or mental health professional. Early intervention can prevent deeper struggles and promote healing.

Embracing the Future: Growth After the Storm

Though the journey is arduous, families can and do emerge stronger. Children learn flexibility, empathy, and the beauty of loving more than one home. Parents discover reserves of strength and the power of their unconditional love.

Cultivating Optimism

Share stories of resilience. Celebrate small victories. Remind children—and yourself—that storms pass, and sunlight returns.

Conclusion

Surviving the storm of separation and divorce requires courage, patience, and compassion. The path is rocky, but with intentional care, children and parents alike can find their footing, rebuild, and eventually thrive. In time, the tempest quiets, and the horizon opens to new beginnings—proof that, even in the aftermath, families can find peace and joy once more.

CHAPTER 1

COURTSHIP AND DATING GAME

(Courtship is the traditional dating period before engagement and Marriage (or long-term commitment if marriage is not allowed). It is an alternative to arranged marriages in which the couple or group does not meet before the wedding. One way courtship varies is in the duration; courting can take days or years.

The institution of marriage is likely to continue but some previous patterns of marriage will become outdated as new patterns emerge. Cohabitation contributes to the phenomenon of people getting married for the first time at a later age than was typical in earlier generations (Glezer, 1991). Furthermore, marriage will continue to be delayed as more people place education and career ahead of 'settling down'. Courtship varies both by time period and by region of the world. One way courtship varies in the duration, courting can take days or years. In the United Kingdom, a poll of 3,000 engaged or married couples suggested an average between first meeting and engagement of 2 years and 11 months. (Lumen Learning, Courses)

Dating is a casual time of fun and getting acquainted. For this reason, the family has always encouraged group dates, several couples going to a ball game. Dating has nothing in view but simple enjoyment and getting acquainted with members of the opposite sex. In a sense dates are fact finding missions. Going steady is a prelude to engagement, it is courtship. Dating can naturally lead to courtship. This will take place when the field is narrowed and considerable fact finding has taken place. It has often been said every date is a potential mate. This is true, the dating process should have been the objective of screening out the characters you detested from each other.

HOW COURTSHIP DIFFERS FROM DATING

DATING	COURTSHIP
Often casual, may not aim at marriage	Always intentional, focused on marriage
Can involve multiple partners over time	Usually exclusive and serious
Driven by fun, attraction, or exploration	Driven by commitment and long-term vision

Cultural Perspectives

- In some cultures, courtship is formal and involves family approval or arranged meetings.
- In others, it's informal and private, where the couple independently decides their future.
- Across traditions, the common thread is preparing for marriage through intentional relationship-building.

In short: Courtship before marriage is a purposeful relationship stage where couples test compatibility, strengthen emotional bonds, and prepare for lifelong commitment. It's the bridge between attraction and marriage, ensuring the decision to wed is thoughtful and well-grounded.

Courtship is an important phase before marriage. Below are some of the reasons:

1. Getting to Know Each Other: Courtship provides an opportunity for individuals to get to know each other's personalities, values, beliefs, and life goals. This understanding is crucial for determining compatibility and shared visions for the future.
2. Building Emotional Connection: It allows couples to build a deeper emotional connection, which forms the foundation of a strong and healthy relationship. This connection is essential for navigating the challenges and changes that life may bring.
3. Assessing Compatibility: Through courtship, couples can assess their compatibility in various aspects such as lifestyle preferences, religious beliefs, financial habits, and family values. This period helps identify potential areas of conflict and whether they can be resolved.
4. Understanding Communication Styles: Good communication is key to a successful marriage. Courtship helps couples learn how to communicate effectively, resolve conflicts, and healthily express their needs and emotions.
5. Building Trust: Trust is a cornerstone of any strong relationship. Courtship allows time for building trust and understanding, ensuring that both partners feel secure and confident in their relationship.

6. Shared Experiences: Spending time together in different situations and settings helps couples understand how they interact in various circumstances, such as dealing with stress, making decisions, and handling disagreements.
7. Family and Social Dynamics: Courtship often involves meeting and interacting with each other's families and social circles. This helps in understanding family dynamics, social expectations, and how each partner fits into the other's life.
8. Testing Long-term Compatibility: Courtship provides a period to see if the relationship can withstand time and challenges. It allows couples to test the strength and durability of their bond before making a lifelong commitment.
9. Clarifying Expectations: During courtship, couples can discuss and align their expectations for the future, including career plans, children, and lifestyle choices. This clarity helps prevent misunderstandings and disappointments later on.
10. Personal Growth: Courtship is also a time for personal growth and self-reflection. It allows individuals to better understand themselves, their desires, and what they are willing to contribute to a partnership.
11. Courtship emphasizes on spiritual compatibility (shared faith), while trying to grasp the will of God for you as you listen and obey your instinct, dreams or any way God or your High power speaks to you. This is because He knows the future, the end from the beginning. Intentionally have a good lasting relationship with God, He would definitely direct you the right way since courtship is a guided process of evaluating love, compatibility, and purpose before making a lifelong commitment.
12. Be watchful, knowing that everyday behavior reveals long-term reality. A good courtship may have challenges but it will not feel like turmoil all the time.
13. Discussions about marriage become clearer over time. Healthy courtship does not stall indefinitely.
Note that, a strong courtship is: Intentional, transparent, spiritually aligned, and steady moving towards a clear decision. While a weak or unhealthy one is: confusing, inconsistent, boundary breaking and directionless.
14. The goal of courtship is not perfection, no one will score perfectly. It is readiness, alignment, and integrity.

If you consistently see:
    i.   7-10 green areas - that is a strong potential
    ii. 4-6 mixed- proceed carefully
    iii. Below that - reconsider seriously
15. Check these important questions and answer them accordingly.
    a. Has this person clearly said they want marriage?
    b. How long have you been talking?
    c. Spiritual life: Do they actively practice their faith?
    d. Do you pray or discuss spiritual things together?
    e. Communication: How do they handle disagreements or misunderstanding?
    f. How responsible are they with money and commitments?
    g. Do you feel peace about them or confusion/anxiety?
    h. Do they respect your limits both emotional and physical?

Courtship is a big engagement to watch out for, so be careful.

Courtship is a critical period for laying the groundwork for a successful marriage. It helps couples build a strong foundation of trust, communication, and understanding, which are essential for a lasting and fulfilling relationship.

MARRIAGE

Marriage is a lifelong partnership built on love, commitment, and mutual support. It's both a personal journey and a social institution that binds two people together emotionally, legally, and often spiritually.

Here's a deeper look at what marriage encompasses:

Core Meaning of Marriage

- Emotional union: Marriage is the weaving together of two lives, where love, trust, and shared dreams form the foundation.
- Commitment: It's a promise to stand by each other through life's highs and lows, offering stability and security.
- Growth together: Partners evolve individually and as a couple, learning from each other and building a shared future.

Spiritual and Cultural Dimensions

- Sacred covenant: In many religious traditions, marriage is seen as a divine bond. For example, Christianity views it as a sacred union reflecting God's design for companionship and love.
- Cultural significance: Across societies, marriage often marks a rite of passage and is celebrated as a cornerstone of family and community life.

Purpose and Benefits

- Companionship: Marriage provides emotional intimacy and a sense of belonging.
- Support system: Spouses offer each other practical help, encouragement, and care.
- Family foundation: It's often the basis for raising children and creating a stable home environment.
- Resilience and growth: Facing challenges together strengthens the bond and fosters personal development.

Communication and Connection

- Healthy communication: Open dialogue, empathy, and vulnerability are key to deepening trust and resolving conflicts.
- Shared rituals: Regular check-ins, celebrations, and traditions help couples feel seen and connected.

A Journey, not a Destination

Marriage isn't just about romance or legal status, it's a dynamic relationship that requires effort, patience, and adaptability. It's about choosing each other, again, through every season of life.

How Marriage Differs Across Cultures

Marriage is a universal institution, but its form and meaning differ dramatically:

- Purpose and Function:
    - In many cultures, marriage is not just about love, it's a strategic alliance between families.
    - For example, in parts of Africa and South Asia, marriages often involve bride prices or dowry, symbolizing economic and social ties.
- Forms of Marriage:
    - Monogamy is common globally, but polygamy (especially polygyny—one-man, multiple wives) is practiced in regions like the Middle East and parts of Africa.
    - Group marriage and polyandry (one-woman, multiple husbands) exist in rare cases, such as among some Tibetan communities.
- Rituals and Customs:
    - In Peru, some Indigenous couples begin with Servin Kuy, living together before formal marriage after childbirth.
    - In India, elaborate multi-day ceremonies reflect religious and regional traditions.
    - In Japan, Shinto weddings emphasize purification and ancestral blessings.
- Legal and Social Recognition:
    - Some cultures recognize common-law marriages or temporary unions, while others require formal religious or civil ceremonies.

Modern Views on Marriage

Marriage today is undergoing a transformation, especially in urban and Western societies:

- Delayed and Declining Marriage Rates:
    - Many people are marrying later or choosing not to marry at all. Cohabitation and single parenthood are more accepted.

- Focus on Personal Fulfillment:
  - Modern couples prioritize emotional intimacy, compatibility, and shared values over social obligation or economic necessity.
- Alternative Relationship Models:
  - Polyamory, parenting partnerships, and long-term cohabitation challenge traditional marriage norms.
- Legal and Social Shifts:
  - Same-sex marriage is now legal in many countries, reflecting broader acceptance of diverse family structures.
  - Gender roles within marriage are more fluid, with shared responsibilities and egalitarian dynamics becoming the norm.

Marriage is no longer a one-size-fits-all institution. It's evolving into a more personalized, inclusive, and dynamic partnership—shaped by culture, values, and individual choice.

Marriage customs have evolved dramatically worldwide, shifting from traditional, family-centered arrangements to more personalized, inclusive, and flexible unions that reflect modern values and lifestyles.

Global Shifts in Marriage Customs

Marriage customs have undergone significant transformations across cultures:

- From Arranged to Love Marriages: In countries like India, arranged marriages are declining as dating apps and social mobility empower individuals to choose their partners.
- Delayed Marriages: Globally, people marry later due to career priorities, education, and financial independence. This trend is especially strong in OECD countries.
- Rise of Cohabitation: In many Western societies, couples increasingly live together without formal marriage, reflecting a shift toward informal partnerships.
- Same-Sex Marriage Legalization: Over 30 countries now recognize same-sex marriage, marking a major shift toward inclusivity and equal rights.

- Decline in Religious Ceremonies: Secular or civil weddings are becoming more common, especially in Europe and North America, as religious affiliation declines.

Evolving Cultural Traditions

Traditional wedding customs are being reimagined or blended with modern elements:

- Henna and Mehndi: In South Asian weddings, the Mehndi ceremony remains popular but is now often combined with Western-style bridal showers.
- Money Dances: Nigerian weddings still feature money dances, but they're now shared widely on social media, adding a modern twist.
- Japanese Sangokushi: The traditional headpiece symbolizing obedience is now worn more for aesthetic than symbolic reasons.
- Western Traditions Globalized: Customs like the white dress, bouquet toss, and first dance have spread globally, often adapted to local cultures.

Statistical Trends

- Marriage Rates: Many countries report declining marriage rates. For example, Colombia has one of the lowest at 1.4 marriages per 1,000 people.
- Divorce Rates: Divorce remains high in many regions, prompting reevaluation of marriage's role and expectations.
- Parenthood Without Marriage: In places like Scandinavia, having children outside of marriage is socially accepted and legally supported.

What This Means

Marriage is no longer a rigid institution, it's a dynamic, evolving partnership shaped by personal choice, cultural heritage, and societal change. Whether through minimalist ceremonies, cross-cultural unions, or alternative relationship models, couples today are redefining what it means to say, "I do."

Marriage, also called matrimony or wedlock, is a socially or ritually recognized union between spouses that establishes rights and obligations between those spouses, as well as between them and any resulting biological or adopted children and affinity (In-laws and other family through marriage). The definition of marriage varies around the world not only between cultures and between religions, but also throughout the history of any given culture and religion, evolving to both expand and constrict in who and what is encompassed, but typically it is principally an institution in which interpersonal relationships, usually sexual., are acknowledged or sanctioned.

In some cultures, marriage is recommended or considered to be compulsory before pursuing any sexual activity. When defining broadly, marriage is considered a cultural universal. A marriage ceremony is known a Wedding. Individuals may marry for several reasons, including legal, social, emotional, spiritual, financial, and religious purposes. Whom they marry may be influenced by socially determined rules. Parental choice and individual desire. In some areas of the world, arranging marriage, child marriage, polygamy, and sometimes forced marriage, may be practiced as a cultural tradition.

Conversely, such practices may be outlawed and penalized in parts of the world out of concerns of the infringement of women's rights, or the infringement of children's rights (both female and male children), and because of international law. Around the world, primarily in developed democracies, there has been a general trend towards ensuring equal rights within marriage for women and legally recognizing the marriages of interfaith, interracial, and same-sex couples. These trends coincide with the broader human rights movement.

Marriage can be recognized by a state, an organization, a religious authority, a tribal group, a local community, or peers. It is often viewed as a contract. When a marriage is performed and carried out by a government institution in accordance with the marriage laws of the jurisdiction, without religious content, it is a civil marriage. Civil marriage recognizes and creates the rights and obligations intrinsic to matrimony before the state.

When a marriage is performed with religious content under the auspices of a religious institution it is a religious marriage. Religious marriage recognizes and creates the rights and obligations intrinsic to matrimony before that religion. Religious marriage is known variously as sacramental marriage in Catholicism, nikah in Islam, issuing in Judaism, and various other names in other faith traditions, each with their own constraints as to what constitutes, and who can enter into, a valid religious marriage.

Some countries do not recognize locally performed religious marriage on its own and require a separate civil marriage for official purposes. Conversely, civil marriage does not exist in some countries governed by a religious legal system, such as Saudi Arabia, where marriages contracted abroad might not be recognized if they were contracted contrary to Saudi interpretations of Islamic religious law. In countries governed by a mixed secular-religious legal system, such as in Lebanon and Israel, locally performed civil marriage also does not exist within the country, preventing interfaith and various other marriages contradicting religious laws from being entered into in the country, however, civil marriages performed abroad are recognized by the state even if they conflict with religious laws (in the case of recognition of marriage in Israel, this includes recognition of not only interfaith civil marriages performed abroad, but also overseas same-sex civil marriages).

The act of marriage usually creates normative or legal obligations between the individuals involved, and any offspring they may produce or adopt. In terms of legal recognition, most sovereign states and other jurisdictions limit marriage to opposite-sex couples and a diminishing number of these permit polygyny, child marriages, and forced marriages. In modern times, a growing number of countries, primarily developed democracies, have lifted bans on and have established legal recognition for the marriages of interfaith, interracial, and same-sex couples. Some cultures allow the dissolution of marriage through divorce or annulment. In some areas, child marriages and polygamy may occur in spite of national laws against the practice.

Since the late twentieth century, major social changes in Western countries have led to changes in the demographics of marriage, with the age of first marriage increasing, fewer people marrying, and more couples choosing to cohabit rather than marry. For example, the number of marriages in Europe decreased by 30% from 1975 to 2005.

Historically, in most cultures, married women had very few rights of their own, being considered, along with the family's children, the property of the husband; as such, they could not own or inherit property or represent themselves legally (see for example coverture). In Europe, the United States, and other places in the developed world, beginning in the late 19th century and lasting through the 21st century, marriage has undergone gradual legal changes, aimed at improving the rights of the wife. These changes included giving wives legal identities of their own, abolishing the right of husbands to physically discipline their wives, giving wives property rights, liberalizing divorce laws, providing wives with reproductive rights of their own, and requiring a wife's consent when sexual relations occur.

These changes have occurred primarily in Western countries. In the 21st century, there continue to be controversies regarding the legal status of married women, legal acceptance of or leniency towards violence within marriage (especially sexual violence), traditional marriage customs such as dowry and bride price, forced marriage, marriageable age, and criminalization of consensual behaviors such as premarital and sex outside marriage (Wikipedia).

FAMILY AND RESPONSIBILITIES

Family responsibilities involve shared roles that foster love, support, and stability across generations. Each member contributes uniquely to the household's emotional, financial, and practical well-being.

Here's a breakdown of how family responsibilities are typically structured and why they matter:

Core Family Roles and Responsibilities

1. Parents (Mother & Father)

    - Provide emotional support and guidance: Nurturing children's development and well-being.
    - Ensure financial stability: Managing income, budgeting, and long-term planning.
    - Set boundaries and discipline: Teaching values, rules, and consequences.
    - Model behavior: Demonstrating respect, responsibility, and resilience.

2. Children

- Respect and obey parents: Following household rules and contributing positively.
- Help with chores: Age-appropriate tasks like cleaning, organizing, or caring for pets.
- Support siblings: Encouraging cooperation and empathy.
- Learn and grow: Focusing on education and personal development.

3. Grandparents

- Offer wisdom and experience: Sharing stories, traditions, and life lessons.
- Provide emotional support: Acting as a stabilizing presence in times of stress.
- Assist with caregiving: Helping with child-rearing or household duties when needed.

4. Siblings

- Foster companionship: Building lifelong bonds through shared experiences.
- Support each other: Emotionally and practically, especially during challenges.
- Collaborate on tasks: Working together to maintain harmony at home.

Intergenerational Responsibilities

According to Pew Research, many Americans believe adult children have a moral obligation to care for aging parents:

- 66% say grown children should provide caregiving for elderly parents.
- 55% believe financial support is also a key responsibility.

Why These Roles Matter

- Creates structure: Clear roles reduce conflict and confusion.

- Builds emotional security: Everyone knows they're valued and supported.
- Promote cooperation: Shared responsibilities foster teamwork and empathy.
- Strengthens society: Families contribute to economic and social stability.

To improve your family dynamics, focus on strengthening communication, setting healthy boundaries, and fostering empathy. These changes build trust, reduce conflict, and create a more peaceful home environment.

Here are some proven strategies to help you cultivate healthier family relationships:

1. Practice Open and Honest Communication

    - Encourage regular check-ins: Create space for everyone to share feelings and concerns.
    - Use "I" statements: Say "I feel…" instead of blaming with "You always…".
    - Listen actively: Show genuine interest and avoid interrupting.

2. Set Clear Boundaries

    - Define personal space and time: Respect each other's need for privacy or alone time.
    - Establish household rules: Make expectations clear and consistent.
    - Say no when needed: Healthy boundaries prevent resentment and burnout.

3. Foster Empathy and Understanding

    - Validate emotions: Acknowledge each other's feelings even if you disagree.
    - Practice forgiveness: Let go of grudges and focus on growth.
    - Celebrate differences: Appreciate each person's unique perspective and personality.

4. Create Peaceful Routines

   - Family meals: Eating together regularly strengthens bonds.
   - Shared activities: Plan game nights, walks, or creative projects.
   - Mindfulness practices: Breathing exercises or quiet time can reduce tension.

5. Address Conflict Constructively

   - Avoid passive aggression: Be direct but kind.
   - Take breaks during heated moments: Step away to cool down before continuing.
   - Seeking resolution, not victory: Aim to understand, not to win.

6. Consider Family Therapy

   - A licensed therapist can help navigate deeper issues like trauma, communication breakdowns, or generational patterns.

Effects of broken family on the children

Having children creates responsibility and will normally motivate parents to carry out their biological psychological, economic and educational functions: to impart care and protection; offer love and health family relationships; provide shelter and material welfare; and promote play and learning Children, combined with the bitterness and anger of a failed relationship, make separation and divorce one of the most terrible experiences endured by adults.

For most divorce is a last resort, not simply to end a nightmare, but sometimes for survival. Broken families can result from separation due to illness, divorce, or other issues. The break-up of a family has many negative impacts on the children. The children are more likely to act out against siblings, biological parents, or stepparents.

Children also develop emotional issues, such as anger, resentment, loneliness, and depression, due to the change in the family unit. Children involved in broken families are also more likely to engage in early sexual activities. With growing economic indecency of women in many regions, it is possible for them to consider raising their children alone. Divorce is also common in areas of high unemployment, rapid urbanization, and social change. Divorce does not indicate a loss of belief in marriage—many divorces remarry—but second and third marriages have even higher incidences of breakdown.

However, marital breakdown is often followed by moving to a new area, changing jobs, and starting a new family. These developments are often used as a pretext for losing touch with children from a previous marriage.

We should all recognize that successful family life is neither enforced dependency, nor isolated individualism, but interdependence within families, this implies a relationship between equal gender and generation. Within communities, social institutions should support families enough to empower them but not trap them in dependency. Like everything else in nature, the family is subject to continuous change. That which is static in nature, dies.

Children grow up, parents grow old, and other children are born. We know about the endless cycle of life, and it is the glory of the family that it is the logical team to make the best and face the worst of what this world has to offer. It is a practical example of the necessary interdependence of humans, able, ideally, to counter most vicissitudes and even to accept generalizations and platitudes with that necessary pinch of salt.

CHAPTER 2

THE CONCEPT OF FAMILIES

In the United States the concepts of family have changed during the past two generations. During the latter half of the 20th century in the United States, the proportion of married couples with children shrank—such families made up only 24 percent of all households in 2000(Fields and Casper 2001). The idea of family has come to signify many familiar arrangements, including blended families, divorced single mothers or fathers with children, never married women with children, cohabiting heterosexual partners, and gay or lesbian families (Bianchi and Casper, 2000).

The increase in single-mother families, which typically have greater per-person expenses and less earning power, may help to explain why, in the general prosperity of the last half of the 2oth century, the percentage of children living in the poorest families almost doubled, rising from 15 to 28 percent (Bianchi and Casper 2000). Bengtson (2001) asserts that relationships involving three or more generations increasingly are becoming important to individuals and families, that these relationships increasingly are diverse in structure and functions, and that for many Americans, multi-generational bonds are important ties for well-being and support over the course of their lives.

FAMILY IS LIKE AN ECOSYSTEM

Understanding the Interconnectedness of Family Life

The notion that "family is like an ecosystem" is a profound metaphor, rich with meaning and insight. Just as an ecosystem is a network of living organisms intricately connected to each other and to their physical environment, a family is a web of individuals, each with unique roles, needs, and influences, existing within a shared space and bound by relationships. To explore this metaphor is to unlock a deeper appreciation for the dynamic, ever-evolving nature of family life, as well as the delicate balance required to sustain its health and harmony.

The Structure of an Ecosystem

Before delving into the parallels, it is helpful to recall what constitutes an ecosystem. In biology, an ecosystem includes all the living things (plants, animals, microorganisms) in a given area, interacting with each other and with their non-living environments (weather, earth, sun, soil, climate, atmosphere). Each organism plays a role—be it as producer, consumer, decomposer, or otherwise—and their interactions create cycles of energy, nutrients, and life itself.

Similarly, a family is composed of individual parents, children, sometimes grandparents, aunts, uncles, or other extended relations with a specific place and contribution. The household is a shared environment, and the family's culture, traditions, habits, and resources constitute its climate and atmosphere.

Roles and Relationships

In an ecosystem, each organism plays a role that supports the greater whole. Trees provide oxygen and shelter, bees pollinate flowers, fungi decompose dead matter to release nutrients back into the soil. The relationships are reciprocal and complex; one species' well-being often depends on another's actions.

Likewise, within a family, each member plays distinct roles. Parents may be likened to the roots of a great tree—offering stability, nourishment, and grounding values. Children, like young shoots or fledgling animals, rely on care and guidance to grow and flourish. Extended family members add diversity and support, much as various species enhance the resilience of an ecosystem.

The health of the family depends on the strength and clarity of these roles, but also on the fluidity with which members adapt to changing conditions. Just as a forest adapts to the seasons, a family adapts to the chapters of life—birth, growth, adolescence, aging, and loss.

Interdependence and Balance

Central to every ecosystem is the principle of interdependence. Remove a single species—like bees from a meadow—and the consequences ripple outward, often in unexpected ways. The meadow may lose its flowers, the animals that depend on those flowers may dwindle, and the entire system is weakened.

In family life, this interdependence is equally vital. The well-being of each member affects the group. When one person is in distress, the ripple effects can be felt throughout the family. When someone thrives, their joy and energy uplift others. This interconnectedness means that communication, empathy, and cooperation are not just ideals, but necessities for a healthy family ecosystem.

Balance is also crucial. In nature, equilibrium is maintained through feedback loops and adaptation. Predators and prey, for example, keep each other's populations in check. If one grows too numerous, the balance tips, and both suffer.

In families, balance is about ensuring that no one person's needs consistently outweigh the others'. It means that responsibilities and resources are shared, that each voice is heard, and that power is neither hoarded nor abused. This equilibrium is delicate and must be continually maintained through dialogue, compromise, and compassion.

Change, Growth, and Resilience

Ecosystems are not static. They change with the seasons, adapt to storms and droughts, recover from disasters, and sometimes transform entirely. These changes can be gradual or sudden, destructive or regenerative.

Families, too, are in constant motion. New members arrive—through birth, marriage, or adoption—while others depart. Children grow up and leave home; elders age and sometimes require greater care. The family may face challenges, a job loss, illness, or conflict. How a family responds to these events defines its resilience.

Resilient ecosystems recover from disturbance through diversity and cooperation. A meadow with many species is more likely to survive a harsh winter than one with only a few types of plants. Similarly, families that value flexibility, openness, and mutual support are better equipped to weather life's storms. They draw strength from their variety of perspectives and skills, and from their shared commitment to one another's well-being.

Communication: The Flow of Energy

In nature, energy flows through an ecosystem as sunlight is transformed by plants, consumed by animals, broken down by decomposers, and cycled back into the earth. This flow is essential to life and growth.

Communication is the life force of the family ecosystem. It fosters understanding, resolves conflict, and creates intimacy. Honest, open, and respectful exchanges keep the system healthy; when communication breaks down, misunderstandings and resentment can take root, weakening the family's foundation.

Just as an ecosystem's health can be measured by the vitality of its cycles, a family's health can often be gauged by the quality of its communication.

Boundaries and Resources

Every ecosystem has boundaries—physical and ecological—that define and protect it. These boundaries prevent harmful intrusions and help regulate the use of resources.

Families, too, need boundaries: rules, routines, and limits that preserve individual well-being and create a sense of safety. These boundaries should be flexible enough to allow growth and change, but firm enough to give structure and predictability. When boundaries are respected, trust flourishes.

Resources—time, money, energy, attention—must also be managed wisely. In an ecosystem, resources are recycled, shared, and sometimes scarce. In families, the wise stewardship of resources is a collective responsibility. Overuse, neglect, or exploitation can lead to depletion and conflict, just as overharvesting can collapse an ecosystem.

Cultural Diversity and Adaptation

Biodiversity is a hallmark of a healthy ecosystem; it ensures resilience and adaptability in the face of change. In families, cultural diversity, whether through backgrounds, beliefs, or interests—can enrich daily life and strengthen the group's ability to adapt.

Embracing differences, rather than suppressing them, leads to a more vibrant and robust family ecosystem. It encourages creativity, fosters tolerance, and prepares members to thrive in a diverse world.

Feedback and Learning

Ecosystems respond to feedback; when something is out of balance, corrective mechanisms often arise. Families, too, benefit from regular reflection and learning. This might take the form of family meetings, open conversations, or simply checking in with one another. Mistakes and conflicts are inevitable, but they are also opportunities for growth. Just as nature adapts and evolves, families can use feedback to learn, heal, and improve.

The Cycles of Life

Finally, both ecosystems and families are shaped by cycles—of day and night, of the seasons, of generations. There are moments of abundance and scarcity, growth and rest, joy and sorrow. Recognizing and honoring these cycles helps families embrace change, cherish each stage, and remain grounded in their shared humanity.

Conclusion: Nurturing the Family Ecosystem

To see family as an ecosystem is to recognize the beauty and complexity of our closest relationships. It is to appreciate that each person matters, that each interaction affects the whole, and that harmony is an ongoing process. Nurturing the family ecosystem requires intention, attention, and care. It means listening deeply, sharing generously, honoring differences, and working together in pursuit of collective well-being. When families embrace their interconnectedness, they become resilient, adaptive, and profoundly nurturing mirroring the breathtaking wisdom and balance found in the natural world. Just as an ecosystem is more than the sum of its parts, so too is a family. In their unity and diversity, their change and continuity, families echo the elegant complexity of life itself—a living system, ever-changing, deeply connected, and full of possibility.

CHAPTER 3

EXCITEMENT IN MARRIAGE

Family is a universal phenomenon. The Family is the oldest, most fundamental, and most enduring of all human institutions. It is the cornerstone of society and our personal lives. It is the source of the new generation, of population growth or control, and of primary childcare. It meets the basic human needs of food and shelter, care for elderly and disabled people, creates wealth and provides large, unrecognized economic services.

Family means socialization, education and transmitting culture, tradition, and skills. The family can profoundly influence our human potential and happiness by the care it offers in our youth.

All our lives we turned to it for love and shared values, for support in good times or bad, and as a reference point that gives meaning to our experience. We learn from family contact throughout our lives: each important experience, such as marriage, having children or retiring, brings new patterns of behavior with it. Learning is most intense during infancy and childhood. The mother is normally the principal teacher of the very young child, at least until weaning. But as the infants' horizons expand, so other people begin to have a growing influence. Older siblings, especially sisters, are important because often they care for the young child. Marriage is a socially recognized union of a man and woman as husband and wife which was instituted by God. It legitimizes sexual access and brings procreation which ensures the continuity of lineage.

THE NORMAL LIFE

It has been so good getting married and everything falling in place as expected. Being mature to marry, meeting loved one, dating, getting to meet with each other's family members and formalizing marriage as the culture would have it. Quite an interesting and exciting process where all relations that have helped in your growing up are brought into the picture. When the rites performance are completed, couples relax and form their nuclear family.

As little your finance might be as young beginners, you wouldn't mind as long as you live together, you begin to manage, face your responsibilities and to make ends meet Much of human activity is directed towards the realization of personal aims and ambitions, especially in terms of marriage, the maintenance of the home and the establishment of a family. It would seem a much more valid interpretation that man works to eat and to provide a living for his dependents and much of his youthful efforts is devoted to acquiring such defendants.

The family has evolved, and for thousands of years it has adapted to a constantly changing world. Families vary so much within regions and among cultures. There is no simple view of the family: no universal definition. Most of us assume we know exactly what family is. We might say that it is a household, a group of people who live together under the same roof and who are related.

A family is not always tied to one place and to one time. A family may split between households. The family exerts a powerful influence over its members, requiring them to respect and preserve the blood line, conserve family tradition and class, and to protect the family's reputation. Our ancestry has considerable bearing on our expectations in life. The ability of the family to control destiny stretches across the generations: some believe it stems from the dead. Ancestral cults are important in many societies. We all are fascinated with our origins—our 'Roots'. Some people travel halfway across the world, at great expense, to trace ancestors and draw up a family tree.

Economic, technological and social developments are having a powerful impact on families. A growing number of couples do not have children: perhaps as many as a third of families have only one parent, (and some center on the partnership of two adults of the same sex) Exhibiting caring values within the family is the surest way to protect and promote the rights and welfare of individual members. The health and wellbeing of young children, for example, is dramatically improved by teaching parents about birth spacing, hygiene, good nutrition, and safety within the home. Informed parents can help prevent disability, alcohol and drug addiction, violence and neglect.

They can also cater for the special needs of disabled members by learning basic rehabilitation techniques. Since women are primarily responsible for child rearing and domestic matters, most family policies and information on family welfare is targeted at them. But programs to involve men in family life are badly needed, if only to ensure the fair distribution of responsibility.

COMPANIONSHIP

This is to avoid loneliness because there are lots of psych-social problems and emotional disturbances that can emanate from a matured man or woman that is staying alone. Everybody needs a friend, a partner, someone to lean on, to talk to, a person that can be dependent upon in times of need, a trusted tier.

This is the real purpose of marriage. Husband and wife should be true friends that manifest loyalty and faithfulness to the last among themselves. A partner that can be leaned on, dependable, trust for this is the purpose of marriage. This partnership is meant to last for a lifetime. The imperative is that you are to leave your original family where you belong to join with the family of your spouse (partner). For this great miracle to take place, there must be a pre-requisite which is 'LOVE' that creates attraction amongst you, but this love must be a genuine one in order to empower you to take this giant step of life. Love is a powerful emotion felt for another person manifesting itself in deep affection, it attracts, magnetizes and it involves deep sexual expression of one another. The spouse delighting in cheating—adultery due to migration or whatever the case may be is a very serious issue in marriage.

Healing from infidelity in marriage takes time, longer, probably, than it did to build the relationship in the first place. Trust is gone, and it might be rebuilt, one act of faith at a time. Even if your mate has forgiven what you did, that doesn't mean he or she will ever forget that you strayed. Marriage is not all about sex and children but also companionship.

Companionship is one of the important basic needs of man. A man is motivated when he feels trusted and respected. Man/woman wants more than anything a soul mate and friend, someone loving, caring, and affectionate. Someone tender to talk to and have fun with. Someone who can be there for you, take interest in the things you do, trust, respect, be loyal and admire you. The ideal companion would focus on your good qualities more than your faults. Someone you could share your feelings, thoughts, interests and whole being. Someone you can relate and listen to with excitement without boundaries.

COMPANIONSHIP BEFORE MARRIAGE

The Importance of Companionship

Companionship before marriage offers individuals a foundation of support, understanding, and mutual respect. It fosters emotional intimacy, allowing partners to learn about each other's values, goals, and personalities in depth.

Building Trust and Communication

Spending time together prior to marriage helps to develop trust and open communication. Through shared experiences, individuals gain insight into each other's strengths, challenges, and approaches to problem-solving.

Establishing Shared Values

Companionship enables partners to explore compatibility and common interests. This period is often marked by discussions about future aspirations, lifestyle preferences, and beliefs, contributing to a strong and unified partnership.

Preparing for Marriage

The companionship stage serves as preparation for marriage, laying the groundwork for a lasting and fulfilling relationship. It allows for the growth of emotional bonds and the cultivation of mutual respect, which are essential for a successful marriage.

COMMITMENT IN MARRIAGE

Husbands and wives who are committed to their marriage view it as a permanent bond, and that creates a sense of security between them. Each spouse is confident that the other will honor the union, even in difficult times. Some couples feel compelled to stay together because of social or family pressure. Far better, however, is a sense of commitment that is based on mutual love and respect. If you are committed to your marriage, you allow yourself to be wronged. You are quick to forgive and quick to apologize. You view problems as obstacles, not as deal breakers. – Micah.

"When confronted with problems, spouses without commitment are likely to conclude, we just weren't made for each other' and look for ways to get out of the marriage. Many people go into marriage knowing that they have a 'fallback plan"—divorce. When people enter marriage already thinking about the possibility of divorce, their commitment is lacking right from the start" – Jean.

Solution

You could ask yourself:

- Do you find yourself regretting that you married your spouse?
- Do you daydream about being with someone else?
- Do you say things such as "I'm leaving you"? Or "I'm going to find someone who appreciates me?"

If you answered yes to one or more of those questions, now is the time to strengthen your commitment. Ask yourself: Has the level of commitment in our marriage decreased? If so, why?

What steps can we take now to strengthen our commitment? Way out.

- Write an occasional love note to your spouse.
- Show your commitment by displaying photos of your spouse on your desk at work.
- Phone your spouse each day while you are at work or apart.

TEAMWORK

When there is teamwork in a marriage, a husband and wife are like pilots and copilots with the same flight plan. Even when challenges arise, each spouse thinks in terms of 'we' rather than 'me'. Marriage is not a solo act. Husband and wife must work together to make it successful. – Christopher.

When a conflict arises a husband and wife who are not a team will tend to attack each other rather than the problem. Minor issues will turn into major obstacles. Imagine a tennis inarch with two of you on opposite sides of the net. Instead, what practical steps can you take to join your spouse so that you are both on the same team dancing? Instead of thinking, 'How can I win?' think, "How can we both win?" Forget about who is right and who is wrong. That isn't as important as having peace and unity in your marriage. – Ethan.

RESPECT

Respectful spouses care about each other even during a disagreement. "These couples don't get gridlocked in their separate position," says the book Ten Lessons to Transform Your Marriage. "Instead, they keep talking with each other about conflicts. They listen respectfully to their spouses' perspectives and find compromises that work for both sides." To respect your wife means that you appreciate her and you don't want to do anything that would damage her or your marriage. – Brian.

Check

Ask yourself:

- How often did I criticize my spouse, and how often did I give her a compliment?
- In what specific ways did I show respect for my spouse?

- What actions and words would help each of you feel respected?
- What actions and words make each of you feel disrespected?

To respect your husband means showing it by your actions that you value him and that you want him to be happy. It isn't always a grand gesture; sometimes a series of small acts can demonstrate genuine respect. – Megan.

In the end, it is not a matter of whether you view yourself as respectful or not; it is a question of whether your spouse feels respected. Be compassionate, tender, kind, humble, mild and patience are important.

THE ESSENCE OF RESPECT IN A MARITAL RELATIONSHIP

The Foundation of Enduring Partnership

Introduction

In the intricate tapestry of marriage, respect is a thread that weaves together diverse elements into a harmonious whole. While love often takes center stage in discussions about marital happiness, it is respect that forms the enduring foundation upon which lasting relationships are built. Without respect, love can falter, giving way to miscommunication, resentment, and emotional distance. When respect flourishes, however, it nurtures trust, intimacy, and mutual growth, allowing both partners to thrive individually and as a couple.

Understanding Respect in Marriage

Respect in a marital relationship extends far beyond mere politeness or courteous behavior. It is a deep-seated recognition of each partner's intrinsic worth, unique perspectives, and personal boundaries. Respect means valuing your partner not for what they provide, but for who they are, appreciating both their strengths and imperfections.

At its core, respect encompasses:

- Listening without judgment or interruption
- Honoring boundaries, both emotional and physical
- Valuing opinions, even in the face of disagreement
- Acknowledging contributions and efforts
- Demonstrating empathy and understanding

The Role of Communication

Effective communication is the lifeblood of respect in marriage. When partners feel heard and understood, they are more likely to feel valued and respected. This means engaging in active listening, which involves giving your full attention, reflecting back what you've heard, and withholding immediate judgments or solutions. Speaking openly about feelings, needs, and concerns, while using "I" statements rather than accusatory language, also fosters an environment where respect can flourish. For example, saying "I feel overwhelmed when the household chores pile up" is more respectful and constructive than "You never help around the house." The former invites dialogue and understanding, while the latter can trigger defensiveness and hurt.

Maintaining Individuality

Respect in marriage also requires honoring each other's individuality. While marriage joins two lives, it does not erase the uniqueness of each partner. A respectful relationship encourages personal growth, the pursuit of interests and friendships outside marriage, and the freedom to express differing opinions. This respect for individuality helps prevent codependence and fosters a healthy interdependence, where both partners remain strong and fulfilled as individuals while sharing their lives together.

Resolving Conflict with Respect

Disagreements are inevitable in any close relationship. What distinguishes strong marriages is not the absence of conflict, but the presence of respectful conflict resolution. This means disagreeing without degrading or belittling one another, avoiding sarcasm or contempt, and refraining from bringing up past grievances as weapons.

Instead, partners should strive to:

- Address issues promptly, rather than letting resentment simmer.
- Focus on the issue at hand, not on attacking character.
- Seek common ground and compromise.
- Apologize sincerely when in the wrong.
- Forgive and let go of grudges.

Approaching conflict with curiosity—seeking to understand rather than to win—can turn disagreements into opportunities for greater understanding and intimacy.

Supporting Each Other's Goals

A respectful marriage is one in which both partners feel supported in their dreams and ambitions. Whether it's pursuing further education, building a career, or nurturing a creative passion, encouragement from a spouse can make all the difference. This support signals a belief in your partner's abilities and aspirations, and it reflects trust in their decision-making. At the same time, it's important to communicate openly about how each person's goals fit into the shared life of the couple, and to find ways to balance individual growth with collective well-being.

Respecting Boundaries

Healthy marriages are built on clear, respected boundaries. These boundaries may involve time, privacy, relationships with friends or family, or personal values. Openly discussing boundaries and honoring them—without guilt-tripping or manipulation—demonstrates deep respect for your partner's autonomy and well-being. For example, respecting a partner's need for alone time after a stressful day, or their desire to maintain certain friendships, strengthens trust and prevents resentment.

Expressing Appreciation and Gratitude

Daily gestures of appreciation are powerful affirmations of respect. Simple acts—thanking your partner for making dinner, acknowledging their hard work, or expressing gratitude for their emotional support—reinforce a sense of being valued and seen.

These acknowledgments should be sincere and specific. Instead of generic praise, noting "I really appreciate how you handled that difficult conversation with your family" carries more meaning and impact.

Dealing with Change and Challenges

Life inevitably brings change—career shifts, health issues, the arrival of children, or the loss of loved ones. How couples navigate these changes can reveal the strength of respect in their relationship. During difficult times, respect is demonstrated through patience, flexibility, and unwavering support. Rather than blaming or withdrawing, partners can face challenges as a team, reaffirming their commitment to one another's well-being, and adapting together to new circumstances.

Respect and Intimacy

Mutual respect lays the groundwork for emotional and physical intimacy. When partners feel safe, accepted, and understood, they are more likely to share their deepest thoughts and feelings, and to maintain a satisfying physical connection. Disrespect, on the other hand—manifested through criticism, neglect, or disregard for consent—erodes trust and intimacy.

The Erosion of Respect: Warning Signs

A lack of respect can take many forms. Common warning signs include:

- Frequent interruptions or dismissals during conversations.
- Contemptuous language or sarcasm.
- Ignoring or invalidating feelings.
- Repeated boundary violations.
- Disregard for your partner's time, interests, or relationships.

Recognizing these signs early allows couples to address issues before they become entrenched patterns.

Cultivating Respect in Everyday Life

Respect is not a static quality; it must be cultivated intentionally and consistently. This can involve:

- Regular check-ins about feelings and needs.
- Setting aside quality time for one another.
- Practicing active listening and empathy.
- Celebrating each partner's achievements, big or small.
- Apologizing and forgiving generously.

These daily practices reinforce a climate of respect and strengthen the marital bond.

Conclusion

Respect is both the soil in which love takes root and the sunlight that helps it grow. In a marital relationship, it is the assurance that each person's voice matters, that boundaries will be honored, and that differences are not only tolerated but cherished. Through mindful communication, empathy, and ongoing appreciation, couples can build a partnership where both individuals feel valued, understood, and empowered to flourish—together and apart. When respect is at the heart of marriage, it becomes an enduring source of strength, resilience, and joy.

FORGIVENESS

To forgive means that you let go of an offense and any feelings of resentment it may have caused. Forgiveness does not require that you minimize the wrong or pretend it never occurred. Forgive freely and as many times you are wronged. "When you love someone, you look past that person's imperfections and instead see the person that he or she is trying to become." – Aaron.

If you hold on to resentment, you can harm yourself physically and emotionally—you can also damage your marriage. "One time my husband apologized for something that hurt me deeply. It was hard for me to forgive him. I eventually did, but I regret that I didn't do it sooner. It put an unnecessary strain on our relationship," – Julia.

When you are offended, do not attribute bad motives to your spouse. Try to excuse your spouse's behavior, remembering that "we all stumble many times". It's easy to forgive when we're both at fault, but it's more difficult when the offense seems one-sided. Accepting an apology and forgiving takes true humility. – Kimbeily.

If you hold unto resentment, you can harm yourself physically and emotionally—you can also damage your marriage.

THE PROFOUND EFFECTS OF FORGIVENESS IN LIFE

Understanding How Letting Go Transforms Mind, Body, and Relationships

Forgiveness is a powerful act that involves deciding to release anger or resentment toward someone, regardless of whether they deserve it. Although often viewed as benefiting others, forgiveness mainly transforms the person who chooses to forgive.

Psychological Benefits of Forgiveness

Alleviation of Negative Emotions

Forgiveness frees us from anger and resentment, improving mental health and well-being. Research shows that those who forgive experience less anxiety, depression, and stress, making room for greater peace and emotional balance.

Improved Self-Esteem and Empowerment

Forgiving is an active way to regain autonomy, showing we are not shaped by others' actions. This perspective strengthens self-worth and emotional control, helping people shift from victimhood to empowerment.

Enhanced Emotional Intelligence

The process of forgiving requires introspection, empathy, and a willingness to understand both ourselves and those who have wronged us. This journey cultivates emotional intelligence, deepens our capacity for compassion, and sharpens our ability to navigate complex interpersonal dynamics.

The Physical Health Benefits of Forgiveness

Reduced Stress and Inflammation

Harboring grudges is not only an emotional weight; it can take a tangible toll on the body. Chronic anger and emotional distress trigger the body's stress response, releasing hormones that can lead to increased blood pressure, heart rate, and inflammation. Over time, this can contribute to a range of health problems, including cardiovascular disease and weakened immune function. In contrast, forgiveness has been linked to lower cortisol levels, improved heart health, and a stronger immune system.

Better Sleep

Unresolved anger and rumination can interfere with restful sleep. Forgiveness helps quiet the mind, allowing for deeper and more restorative rest. People who forgive tend to experience fewer insomnia-related problems and report better overall sleep quality.

Longevity and Vitality

The cumulative health advantages associated with forgiveness—lower stress, reduced inflammation, and better sleep—may contribute to a longer, healthier life. While more research is needed, evidence suggests that those who practice forgiveness are more likely to thrive physically as well as emotionally.

Social and Relational Effects of Forgiveness

Rebuilding Broken Relationships

Human relationships are intricate and imperfect; misunderstandings and betrayals are almost inevitable. Forgiveness provides a pathway to healing rifts, restoring trust, and renewing connections. It opens the door to honest dialogue, mutual understanding, and the possibility of reconciliation. Even when relationships cannot or should not be restored, forgiveness can bring closure and peace.

Creating a Culture of Compassion

Forgiveness is contagious. When one person extends forgiveness, it can inspire others to do the same, fostering an environment of empathy and kindness. This ripple effect can transform families, workplaces, and communities, laying the groundwork for more harmonious and supportive social networks.

Breaking the Cycle of Hurt

Unforgiven grievances often perpetuate cycles of retaliation and alienation. By choosing forgiveness, individuals can interrupt this pattern, preventing further harm and setting a precedent for healthier interactions. Forgiveness does not erase the past but redefines the future.

Spiritual Benefits of Forgiveness

A Path to Inner Peace

Many philosophical and spiritual traditions hold forgiveness as a central virtue. Whether through religious teachings or secular ethics, forgiveness is seen as essential for personal growth and moral development. It is a practice that enables the soul to unburden itself and move toward serenity.

Transcending the Self

Forgiveness invites us to rise above personal grievances, recognizing the shared humanity of all people. It is an acknowledgment of imperfection—ours and others'—and a willingness to choose understanding over judgment. This transcendence can foster a sense of connection to something greater than oneself.

Obstacles to Forgiveness

While the benefits of forgiveness are plentiful, the path is rarely easy. Common barriers include:

- Misperceptions: Confusing forgiveness with condoning or forgetting the offense.
- Pride and Ego: Reluctance to let go of a perceived moral high ground.
- Lack of Empathy: Difficulty seeing the situation from another's perspective.
- Ongoing Harm: Forgiveness is more complicated when the hurt is repeated or unresolved.

Overcoming these obstacles often requires patience, support, and sometimes professional guidance. Self-forgiveness can be especially challenging, yet it is fundamental for healing and moving forward.

Cultivating

Reflect and Acknowledge

Begin by identifying the hurt and acknowledging the pain. This honest self-reflection lays the groundwork for letting go.

Empathize with the Offender

Try to see the situation from the perspective of the person who caused harm. This does not excuse their behavior but can help release resentment.

Express Your Feelings Safely

Find healthy ways to process and express emotions, such as journaling, talking with a trusted friend, or seeking support from a counselor or spiritual advisor.

Set Boundaries if Needed

Forgiveness does not require continued exposure to harmful behavior. Protecting oneself is an essential part of the process.

Commitment

Forgiveness is a deliberate choice, sometimes made repeatedly. Try to replace ruminative thoughts with affirmations of release and peace.

Evidence of Forgiveness in Action

Forgiveness has been shown to greatly benefit mental and physical health. Studies, such as those from Stanford University's Forgiveness Project, indicate that practicing forgiveness can be crucial for healing after trauma or loss.

In families divided by past conflicts, forgiveness can restore peace and togetherness. On a larger scale, collective acts of forgiveness—like South Africa's Truth and Reconciliation Commission—have supported national recovery and progress.

Forgiveness is an ongoing practice with significant benefits. It helps restore well-being, mend relationships, and foster compassion. By forgiving, we let go of past hurts and create space for greater health, happiness, and connection.

Jesus Christ taught forgiveness, encouraging us to forgive others as He has forgiven us. The Holy Spirit is pleased when we forgive those who wrong us, making life smoother. Forgiveness brings great joy and is truly valuable.

SHOW APPRECIATION

It's easy to get too comfortable in a relationship, and sometimes that comfort can translate into forgetting to show your partner respect and appreciation. Dr. Edelman says our partners can feel taken for granted if we don't tell them we like what they're doing for us. "It means a lot when you acknowledge the large and small things they do for you," Dr. Edelman says. "Say, 'Thanks for making breakfast today. I really appreciate all the time you saved me. It means a lot because I know you were really busy today.'"

LEARN FROM WHAT YOU THINK IS HIS MISTAKE

Instead of harping on a mental list of things your partner does that secretly drive you crazy, find a way to learn from what makes them different from you. "This resolution will cause you to think outside the box about how you consider a trait or behavior good versus bad," says Kyrss Shane, a LMSW and mental health professional. "It will also challenge you to turn an annoyance into something beneficial, helping you not to be bothered by that trait and helping your partner to not feel that this trait is a negative part of who they are."

GIVE YOUR TIME TO ONE ANOTHER

It's easy to spend a handful of minutes, or even an hour or two, on your phone without even realizing it. But giving your full attention to the screen in front of you, instead of your partner, can lead to problems in the relationship. Jill Murray, Ph.D., a licensed psychotherapist, suggests making next year the year when you both vow to stay off your phones when you're together. So many couples go out to dinner and both of them are face down looking at their phones, absorbed in social media, says Murray. "They are 'liking' other people's lives more than they are liking their partner. Commit to giving your focus and attention to your partner."

HANDLE ARGUMENTS PROPERLY

No couple is immune to arguments, and having a system in place to handle hurt feelings now will strengthen your relationship later. Matthew Mutchler, Ph.D., LMFT, says he often sees couples who have different expectations of how to handle a disagreement. "People get wrapped up in being 'right' or 'fixing' a problem [and] they miss the point," says Mutchler. "Underlying many conflicts is a desire to be heard, understood, and validated. You can tell the quality of a relationship by how they hear and respond to one another. Your partner might just want you to say, 'I understand what you're feeling' without qualifications."

SHARE NEW EXPERIENCES TOGETHER

Relationships thrive when good communication exists, but for that to happen, both people need to know how to speak each other's language. "If you have something emotional to say, try to keep it simple so your partner is less likely to get overwhelmed," says Dr. Susan Edelman, a board-certified psychiatrist. "Use 'I language': Say, 'I feel' rather than 'you always,' which can feel like an accusation. If your partner criticizes you, try to hear their concern even if you feel defensive.

CHAPTER 4

THE EFFECTS OF SEPARATION AND DIVORCE ON CHILDREN AND COUPLES

Understanding Emotional, Social, and Psychological Impacts

Introduction

Separation and divorce mark profound transitions in the lives of families. While the dissolution of a partnership may be the result of irreconcilable differences, the effects reach far beyond the immediate relationship. Children and couples alike experience a complex mix of emotional, psychological, and social consequences. This document explores the multifaceted effects of separation and divorce, offering insight into both immediate and long-term impacts, as well as factors that contribute to resilience and healing.

EFFECTS ON COUPLES

Emotional Turbulence

The process of separating from a life partner is often accompanied by a cascade of emotional responses. For many, there is an initial wave of grief and loss, even if the relationship has become strained or unsatisfying. Individuals may feel anger, guilt, shame, relief, anxiety, or a deep sadness. The intensity and duration of these emotions vary widely depending on the circumstances of the relationship, the reasons for separation, and the personal coping resources of each partner.

Identity and Self-Concept

Couples often find that their identities have become intertwined over the course of their relationship. Separation can lead to a crisis of self—who am I without my partner? This redefinition may be both challenging and liberating. Some individuals embark on a journey of self-discovery, seeking new interests and friendships, while others may feel lost or uncertain about their future.

Social Consequences

The end of a partnership can disrupt social networks. Friends may take sides or drift away. Extended family relationships, especially with in-laws, may become strained. The stigma associated with divorce or separation—though reduced in many societies—still leads to a sense of isolation or exclusion.

Financial Impacts

Divorce frequently brings financial instability. Couples must navigate the division of assets, debts, and responsibilities. The shift from a dual-income household to a single-income situation can mean changes in living standards, housing, employment, and access to resources. As Matthew Fray notes, individuals may experience pain, insecurity and loss of identity. Divorce impacts not only the couple but also those around them. Many people find resilience, drawing on inner strength to move forward, even after such a disruptive event (Matthew Fray, 2022).

Physical and Mental Health

Studies suggest that separated and divorced individuals are at increased risk for health challenges. These can include sleep disturbances, changes in appetite, increased substance use, and a higher prevalence of anxiety and depression. Chronic stress associated with the legal and emotional process can also impact immune function and overall wellbeing.

Pathways to Healing

Despite the difficulties, many individuals find growth and resilience through and after separation. Therapy, supportive social networks, healthy routines, and self-reflection can foster recovery. Over time, some people report increased happiness, personal development, and satisfaction once free from a dysfunctional or unhappy relationship.

EFFECTS ON CHILDREN

Emotional Responses

Children are deeply affected by the separation of their parents. Age, temperament, and the circumstances of the breakup play crucial roles in shaping their reactions. Common emotional responses include sadness, anger, confusion, guilt, and fear. Younger children may blame themselves for the separation, while older children and adolescents may feel betrayed or caught between parents.

Behavioral Changes

Many children demonstrate changes in behavior following a parental separation. These can include withdrawal from social activities, academic decline, aggression, and regression to earlier developmental stages (such as bedwetting or clinginess). Adolescents may rebel, seek risky behaviors, or attempt to exert control in other areas of their lives.

Adjustment and Adaptation

The adjustment period varies from child to child. The quality of the parent-child relationship, the level of conflict between parents, and the stability of their environment are key factors. Children whose parents maintain civility and cooperation generally fare better than those exposed to ongoing conflict or parental alienation.

Impact on Relationships and Trust

Children of separated or divorced parents may struggle with trust and intimacy in their own relationships later in life. Their models of partnership are shaped by their parents' interactions and the resolution of conflict. Some may develop fear of commitment or divorce anxiety, while others may become more resilient and determined to build healthy partnerships.

Academic and Social Development

Disruption in family structure can affect academic performance and social integration. Changing schools, moving homes, or adjusting to new routines can undermine a child's sense of stability. Children may experience bullying, loss of friendships, or difficulty focusing on learning.

Long-Term Effects

Research indicates that while most children eventually adjust to their parents' separation, some experience lingering effects. These may include emotional insecurity, difficulties in future relationships, and increased risk for mental health challenges. However, children who receive emotional support, maintain strong relationships with both parents, and have access to counseling or supportive resources tend to recover more readily.

Protective Factors and Resilience

The presence of protective factors can significantly mitigate the negative effects of separation and divorce on children. These include:

- Consistent, loving relationships with both parents
- Minimal parental conflict, especially in the child's presence
- Stable routines and environments
- Open communication and encouragement to express feelings
- Access to extended family, counselors, or support groups

SPECIAL CONSIDERATIONS

High-Conflict Separations

When separation is accompanied by high levels of conflict, hostility, or legal battles, the negative impacts on children and couples intensify. Children may be exposed to emotional manipulation, pressure to choose sides, or even parental alienation, which can cause lasting psychological harm.

Custody Arrangements

The structure of custody arrangements—whether joint, sole, or shared—can influence the adjustment process. Children benefit most from arrangements that prioritize their best interests, maintain meaningful contact with both parents, and minimize disruption.

Remarriage and Blended Families

The introduction of stepparents and stepsiblings adds another layer of complexity. While some children adapt well, others may feel displaced or anxious about new family dynamics. Successful integration depends on patience, open communication, and respecting the child's need to change at their own pace.

Conclusion

Separation and divorce, while challenging, are not insurmountable obstacles to wellbeing and happiness. Couples often navigate a tumultuous emotional landscape, but many eventually find meaning and growth as they move forward. Children are vulnerable to stress, but with the right support and guidance, resilience is possible. The effects of separation and divorce are deeply personal, shaped by unique family circumstances and individual resources. By acknowledging the challenges and embracing pathways to healing, families can move through transition toward renewal and hope.

CHAPTER 5

NUCLEAR FAMILY

A nuclear household consists of a married couple and their unmarried children, or a single parent and unmarried children, whereas an extended household comprises, in addition to a nuclear family unit, a broader set of kin and sometimes unrelated individuals. This nuclear group is found worldwide, but it is most prevalent in the west where it seems to epitomize the modern family. In a western country such as the UK, little more than a quarter of all households are nuclear families.

Nuclear families are common in industrialized cities, with the advent of Industrialization, adult life expectancy increased, so three generation families become common in towns and cities. In Africa, nuclear families are in the minority, this is because men leave their wife and children in search of money, passion and power. On getting there they are grabbed by younger ladies anxiously looking for already made men.

Having in mind that men are free to marry as many wives as possible but for a woman, one man is enough, you have to stick to your first husband till death do you part, even if he is beating you up you have your children to take care of, you must listen and obey your husband, you can be the first wife which is the only honor you have as a married woman. Tolerant, the elders will tell you.

Once the man goes out, he might not come back to his first wife again, he would pretend to be charmed, forgetful and searching for useless reasons for his actions. The irresponsible man now gives reasons for abandoning his young beautiful wife and children he once loved and suffered with when they had nothing but love for a new illegal cohabitation.

IMPACT OF MIGRATION ON THE NUCLEAR FAMILY

This entails greater reliance by the abandoned and the children, a weakening of wider kinship relationships and a consequent widening of the roles of nuclear family members especially women. (Migration and Family, p.48) Female headship of incomplete nuclear families is common in areas where temporary mobility occurs. In such circumstances women and children must perform tasks naturally done by men. (Naim (53), p.425) found that the extended absences of Minangkabau migrant men from their homes created strains within family and may have been responsible for an unusually high incidence of Oedipus complex among children and of mental disorders among women.

Families of migrant men at the place of origin must adjust not only to the permanent or temporary absence of family members, but also to the influences of the newly acquired money, goods, ideas, attitudes, behavior and innovations transmitted back to them by the movers. This is because the acquired position, money, power have a great influence on the mover, who are dominantly the men.

Migration of the head of the family does lead to the separation of family members, creating a greater dependence on the nuclear family, weakening wider kinship relationships and consequently expanding the roles of nuclear family members, especially the women. Caldwell 8 (21) p. 274) has identified such changes as being critical to the transition from high to low fertility, which requires a reversal of the net flow of wealth. Hattaway (25) p.3) suggests that the mobility induced separation of family members, even for short periods, leads to marital instability and the consequent permanent break-up of the family unit, whereas Gonzalex (21), p.1266) cites several studies of the societies in which the temporary separation of husband and wife has been consistent with marital instability. A high incidence of divorce among the Minangkabau of Western Sumatra has been attributed to high rates of male migration (53) p.426), whereas Lineton (44), p.65) suggests that the low incidence of divorce among the Bugis of Wajo is partly because nuclear families migrate.

Though in more recent years, increased modernization and industrialization has generally led to families becoming more geographically and socially mobile, with the result that extended family ties are shed. Modern industrial and urban living is tending to erode family structures back into the more isolated nuclear form. The more that families become isolated from their grandparents and other relatives, the more they become reliant on state and private support.

Migration of the man/head of the household to another country in search of greener pasture is becoming a big issue in families. The nuclear family is most affected; the wife and children would be left behind to suffer and to take care of themselves. The burden would be on the woman of the house/ wife, this is because she would be depressed hoping for the husband to be back, the extended family would begin to look into her family affairs monitor and control her. They would want to know how she gets the finance for her family needs and begin to label her "a prostitute".

The 'Girl Child' in every family should be educated before giving her out in marriage. If the 'girl child' is educated, she would be able to take care of her family in the absence of the husband.

She stands a better chance of sending her children to school to be well educated because she would have a good job, soon she would catch up with her new role and responsibility as a single parent and head of her family. Having a man or no man in your life does not define whom you are as a person. You have just one life to live, you need to make yourself happy as much as you can.

You should not allow yourself to be put down because of the absence of a man that does not want nor love you. Move on with your life and enjoy it, you have a great destiny to fulfill. Soon the single parent would get used to her new roles and be strong to take care of herself and her children. When men migrate, they begin to form another nuclear family over there and tend to forget their first love, this is ridiculous. It would be like a dream to her, she might fall sick, depressed, crying most of the time, emotionally, socially, psychologically and physically down.

The family is separated, divorced and irreparable. Children are disorganized, growing up without the father figure in their lives which was not what the woman anticipated when she got married. Family disintegration affects children more because the boys would join bad people that would teach them to smoke, fight, become a school dropout and many more ills, while the girls will tend to experiment on sex and thereby have babies without a father when they are babies themselves. These days when a man wants to migrate, he would sit with the wife to discuss, it's either your family goes with you or forget it. Disintegration of families is not the best for the family, church, society, community nor the country.

EFFECTS OF HUSBAND MIGRATION TO ANOTHER COUNTRY WITHOUT HIS NUCLEAR FAMILY

Socioeconomic, Emotional, and Cultural Consequences

Migration, particularly the movement of a husband to a foreign country while the nuclear family remains behind, is a phenomenon that has shaped communities, economies, and family structures for generations. This separation, often driven by the pursuit of better economic opportunities, education, or safety, leaves indelible marks on both the individual who migrates and the family members who stay. The impact of such migration is multifaceted, affecting emotional bonds, financial stability, social dynamics, and even the cultural identity of all involved.

SOCIOECONOMIC IMPACTS

Economic Remittances and Dependency

One of the primary motivations for husband migration is the promise of increased income through employment abroad. Remittances sent home often become a crucial lifeline for families, elevating their standard of living and providing access to better education, healthcare, and housing. These remittances can alleviate poverty, enable business investments, or support extended family networks.

However, this financial inflow can also foster economic dependency within the nuclear family. Over time, the family's income may become overly reliant on the husband's earnings abroad, discouraging other family members from seeking local employment or entrepreneurship. This dependency can be precarious, especially if the migrant faces job loss or economic downturns in the host country.

Shifts in Family Roles and Responsibilities

In the absence of the husband, the spouse left behind often assumes dual roles—as both caregiver and breadwinner. This juggling act can be empowering, fostering resilience and independence, particularly among women who may have had limited autonomy before. Yet, it can also lead to exhaustion, stress, and a sense of overwhelming responsibility as the remaining spouse manages children, household finances, and sometimes elder care single-handedly. Children in such families may need to take on additional responsibilities as well, such as helping with household chores, caring for younger siblings, or even contributing to the family income. This shift can accelerate maturity, but it may also interfere with their academic and social development.

EMOTIONAL AND PSYCHOLOGICAL IMPACTS

Strain on Marital Relationships

Physical distance can strain even the strongest marriages. Daily communication may be limited by time zones, work schedules, or technological barriers. Over time, emotional intimacy may erode, and misunderstandings can multiply in the absence of nonverbal cues. Some couples manage to cultivate trust and emotional connection despite the distance, but others may experience feelings of isolation, jealousy, or uncertainty regarding the future.

Effects on Children

The prolonged absence of a parent can deeply affect children's emotional well-being. Younger children may struggle to understand why their parents are gone, feeling abandoned or unloved. Adolescents, meanwhile, may act out or withdraw emotionally, grappling with resentment or insecurity. While remittances may provide material comfort, they cannot replace the daily presence and emotional support of a parent. In some cases, children may look to extended family members, teachers, or community leaders for guidance and affection.

Mental Health Challenges

Both the migrant husband and the family left behind are at risk for mental health challenges. The husband may face loneliness, homesickness, and the pressures of adapting to a new culture, sometimes in the face of discrimination or exploitation. The spouse and children remaining at home may struggle with anxiety, depression, or chronic stress. Access to mental health resources can be limited, especially in communities where seeking support carries social stigma.

SOCIAL AND CULTURAL IMPACTS

Changes in Community Dynamics

Widespread patterns of male migration can reshape entire communities. Social networks may become more fragmented as nuclear families operate in partial absence. The spouse left behind may find solace and support in extended family or peer groups experiencing similar circumstances yet may also face judgment or stigma—sometimes unjustly accused of failing to maintain family unity.

Cultural Identity and Assimilation

For the migrant, immersion in a new culture may foster personal growth and broaden perspectives. However, it can also lead to cultural dissonance and a sense of being "between worlds." The family at home may retain traditional customs, sometimes causing generational or cultural divides when the family eventually reunites. Children in particular may struggle with hybrid identities if they later join their parents abroad.

Gender Norms and Family Authority

Long-term separation can challenge traditional gender norms. In the husband's absence, the spouse may gain greater authority in decision-making, household management, and social affairs. This shift can be empowering but may also provoke resistance from more traditional relatives or community members. When the husband returns, renegotiating roles and authority within the family can be complex and sometimes contentious.

Education and Aspirations

Children in migrant families often have greater access to educational opportunities, funded by remittances. The hope for a better future can inspire children to excel academically. However, the absence of a parent may also hamper educational progress if emotional distress or increased responsibilities interfere with schoolwork. In some cases, the entire family may eventually migrate, introducing children to new educational systems and expectations, which can be both challenging and enriching.

Long-Term Outcomes and Reunification

Some families are eventually reunited, whether through family sponsorship, permanent settlement, or return migration. Reunification can be a joyful event, but it is not without its challenges. Family members must renegotiate relationships, roles, and routines that have changed during the separation. Children may experience difficulty adjusting to a parent who has become more like a distant figure than a daily presence. For others, migration becomes a long-term or even permanent arrangement, with families maintaining transnational relationships across borders. Advances in communication technologies have made it easier to sustain emotional connections, but the core challenges of physical separation remain.

Conclusion

The migration of a husband to another country without his nuclear family is a decision fraught with complexity. While it can offer significant economic benefits and personal growth, it also incurs emotional, social, and cultural costs. Navigating these challenges requires resilience, adaptability, and, ideally, strong support networks both at home and abroad. Policymakers and community organizations can play a vital role by providing resources, counseling, and opportunities for family reunification that help families weather the disruptions wrought by migration. Ultimately, each family's experience is unique, shaped by their circumstances, strengths, and the bonds that persist across distance.

CHAPTER 6

IMPACT OF SUBSTANCE ABUSE ON FAMILIES

DANGER OF ALCOHOLISM

It is important to understand that families with an alcoholic member 'has alcoholism' in the same way that families with a mental or physical illness are impacted by that illness. Alcoholism regulates all behaviors in family life. Therefore, if the primary regulatory relationship in the family is with alcohol or drugs, then other relationships in the family become secondary and do not prosper as well as in a family without alcohol, tobacco and drug abuse.

THE DANGERS OF ALCOHOLISM IN MARITAL RELATIONSHIPS

Understanding the Impact, Consequences, and Pathways to Healing

Alcoholism, often defined as the chronic and compulsive consumption of alcoholic beverages to the detriment of one's health and social functioning, exerts profound influence not only on the individual who suffers from it but also on those closest to them. Within the sanctity of marriage, where trust, emotional support, and cooperation are the foundation, alcoholism can become a silent intruder, slowly unraveling the very fabric that binds two lives together. This document explores the multifaceted dangers of alcoholism in marital relationships, examining its emotional, psychological, and practical repercussions, as well as avenues for healing and resilience.

The Subtle Infiltration: Alcoholism's Entry into Marriage

No marriage begins with the intention of being torn asunder by addiction. Often, alcohol use starts with innocently a glass of wine at dinner, celebratory toasts, or shared drinks with friends. However, when consumption escalates and dependence forms, the dynamic shifts. The partner grappling with alcoholism may gradually become distant, irritable, or unreliable, and the other partner may find themselves walking on eggshells, trying to predict moods and avoid conflict.

Alcoholism rarely announces itself dramatically; more often, it seeps in, altering routines, priorities, and emotional connections. Hidden bottles, unexplained absences, and broken promises slowly take the place of honesty, reliability, and affection. The partner not struggling with addiction may feel increasingly isolated, resentful, or helpless, setting the stage for the deeper consequences that follow.

Emotional and Psychological Toll

Breach of Trust

One of the first casualties of alcoholism in marriage is trust. Addiction breeds secrecy—lies about drinking, hiding evidence, and denying the seriousness of the problem. The non-addicted partner may feel betrayed, leading to suspicion and accusations. Without trust, communication falters, and emotional intimacy wanes, leaving both partners feeling alone even when together.

Anxiety, Fear, and Uncertainty

Alcoholism is unpredictable. Mood swings, outbursts, and erratic decisions can create an environment of chronic anxiety. The non-alcoholic partner may worry constantly about the state of their spouse, finances, or even their safety. Children, if present, are exposed to this instability, further amplifying the household's stress.

Emotional Neglect and Isolation

As the addicted partner's focus shifts to alcohol, their capacity to offer emotional support diminishes. Shared joys, dreams, and even mundane conversations become rare. The non-addicted partner may begin to feel invisible—present in the relationship but emotionally abandoned.

Depression and Self-Esteem Issues

Partners of people with alcoholism frequently experience depression, either as a direct result of the turmoil or from the erosion of affection and validation. The person struggling with addiction may also suffer from guilt and low self-worth, trapped in a cycle where alcohol is both cause and temporary solution.

Escalation of Conflict and Domestic Violence

Alcohol impairs judgment and reduces inhibitions, making arguments more likely to escalate into heated conflicts. Studies have shown that alcoholism is a significant risk factor for domestic violence; verbal arguments can turn physical, and tempers can flare with devastating consequences. The home, meant to be a place of safety, becomes fraught with tension and danger.

Verbal and Emotional Abuse

Even in the absence of physical violence, alcoholism increases the risk of emotional and verbal abuse. The addicted partner may lash out, blame, or manipulate, while the other may respond with defensive or controlling behaviors. Over time, both individuals may become trapped in destructive patterns of communication.

Physical Safety

In extreme cases, alcohol-fueled rage can lead to physical altercations. The risk of injury, legal problems, or irreversible trauma looms large. Fear may prevent the non-alcoholic partner from seeking help or leaving the relationship, perpetuating the cycle of abuse.

Financial and Practical Consequences

Instability and Insecurity

Alcoholism often leads to financial mismanagement, missed work, job loss, or reckless spending on alcohol. Savings dwindle, bills go unpaid, and debts accumulate. The non-alcoholic partner may be forced to shoulder the family's financial responsibilities, adding to their stress and sense of entrapment.

Neglect of Household and Parental Duties

Routine tasks—paying bills, caring for children, maintaining the home—may fall by the wayside as the addiction worsens. Children, in particular, are at risk; they may experience neglect or even be forced into the role of caregiver to their affected parent.

Social Isolation

Couples dealing with alcoholism may withdraw from friends and extended family, either out of shame or to hide the problem. Social invitations are declined, and support networks shrink, leaving both partners even more isolated and vulnerable.

Impact on Children

If marriage involves children, the dangers become even more pronounced. Children living in a home with alcoholic parents are at increased risk for emotional problems, academic difficulties, and substance abuse in their own futures. Witnessing conflict, neglect, or abuse can cause lasting trauma, shaping a child's relationships and coping mechanisms for years to come.

- Unpredictability and Fear: Children may grow up in an environment of chronic uncertainty, never knowing what mood to expect from their parents.
- Parentification: Children may assume adult responsibilities prematurely, caring for siblings or the addicted parent.
- Long-Term Psychological Impact: The trauma of growing up in an alcoholic household often leads to anxiety, depression, and difficulty forming healthy relationships later in life.

Barriers to Seeking Help

Many couples remain trapped in destructive cycles because of stigma, denial, or fear of judgment. The addicted partner may minimize or rationalize their drinking, while the other may enable the behavior due to guilt or hope for change. Societal pressures, religious beliefs, or economic dependence can make it difficult for either partner to seek help or end the relationship.

Pathways to Healing and Recovery

The dangers of alcoholism in marriage are profound, but recovery is possible. Healing begins with acknowledgment—both addiction and its impacts.

- Open Communication: Honesty about the problem is a first step. Couples counseling or support groups, such as Al-Anon, can provide safe spaces for vulnerable discussion.
- Professional Intervention: Addiction is a medical condition, and treatment may include therapy, rehabilitation programs, or medication.
- Rebuilding Trust: Consistency, transparency, and patience are essential. Rebuilding trust takes time, but with genuine commitment, couples can rediscover intimacy and partnership.
- Establishing Boundaries: The non-addicted partner may need to protect their own well-being, including setting limits or, in some cases, considering separation for safety.
- Restoring Family Function: Family therapy and child-focused interventions can help repair relationships and foster resilience in children.

Conclusion

Alcoholism in marital relationships is a silent destroyer, undermining trust, emotional security, and the very foundation of family. Its dangers ripple outward, affecting not only spouses but children and the broader community. Yet, even in the depths of addiction, hope remains. With courage, support, and professional help, couples and families can break free from the grip of alcoholism and embark on the journey toward healing and renewal. Sobriety is achievable and there is hope.

Denial is an integral component of the abused family homeostasis mechanism, the family will blame factors outside of the family for their problems (i.e. loss of job, lack of money, problems at work/school, arguments with friends). This externalization of blame reflects the powerlessness felt throughout the family system. The chemically dependent member functions to bring the family together as they bond against these outside issues through the crises that are caused by the abuse (Fisher & Harrison, 1997).

Families with substance abuse problems utilize criticism, anger, blame, guilt, and judgment in the family communication process as is seen in the marital day. Parenting is inconsistent, and the boundaries are nuclear and consistently changing (Lowery, 1998). A study shows that the most common consequences were distress at witnessing violence to the other parent or to the home, verbal abuse toward the children, feelings of shame, and taking on caring and protective roles. However, the children were not passive victims and usually took active steps to tackle the drinking or modify its impact.

Many abused families wished they could meet with others in the same position, so they could feel less isolated and learn from each other. There is a need for a network of services with group work, individual counseling, family meditation and educational components to keep the family together and moving forward.

Parental alcoholism appears to create the same type of dysfunction that exists in families with sexual, physical, or emotional abuse. This puts the children in these families at high risk for the development of a variety of stress-related disorders (Kelly & Myers, 1996), including conduct disorders, poor academic performance, and inattentiveness. Children in substance abuse families are socially immature, lack self-esteem and self-efficacy, and have deficits in social skills (Sales, 2000). All this leads to family dysfunction in so many ways, in which case the father moves away, living an irresponsible life and the wife lives as a single mother taking care of the children alone. This is actually a family drama issue.

THE DANGEROUS EFFECTS OF SUBSTANCE USE ON FAMILIES' PROGRESS

How Addiction Disrupts Growth, Stability, and Future Generations

Substance use, whether occasional or chronic, can cast a long shadow over families, eroding the foundations of progress, stability, and hope for future generations. When one or more family members fall prey to addiction—be it alcohol, illicit drugs, or prescription medication—the repercussions ripple outward, touching the lives of every individual within the household. The devastating effects are not confined to the person using substances, but create a web of emotional, financial, and social distress that can stall or even reverse a family's progress across multiple domains.

Emotional Fragmentation and Psychological Trauma

Perhaps the most immediate and insidious impact of substance use lies within the emotional sphere. Families thrive on trust, communication, and mutual support—qualities that addiction undermines at every turn.

- Breach of Trust: Substance use can lead to deception, secrecy, and broken promises. Children may witness a parent's erratic behavior and unreliability, eroding their sense of security and attachment.
- Psychological Distress: Anxiety, depression, and trauma are common among family members living with someone who abuses substances. The unpredictability of addiction fosters chronic stress and emotional instability.
- Conflict and Estrangement: Interpersonal relationships suffer as tempers flare, arguments escalate, and misunderstandings become commonplace. Substance use can breed resentment, anger, and emotional withdrawal, driving wedges between spouses, siblings, and generations.

The cumulative psychological toll can manifest in lifelong mental health challenges, affecting not only immediate family but also the generations that follow.

Disruption of Financial Stability and Socioeconomic Progress

Financial well-being is a cornerstone of family progress, enabling a household to pursue education, healthcare, homeownership, and upward mobility. Substance use places this foundation in jeopardy.

- Lost Income and Employment: Addiction often leads to absenteeism, job loss, and decreased productivity. The affected individual may struggle to maintain stable employment, resulting in reduced household income.

- Increased Expenses: Funds that could be invested in education, savings, or family experiences may be diverted to purchase substances or cover associated legal and medical costs.
- Debt and Financial Instability: Families may accumulate debt to finance an addiction, leading to foreclosure, bankruptcy, and loss of assets. The downward financial spiral triggered by substance use can impede a family's ability to plan for the future, invest in their children's education, or break the cycle of poverty.

Impact on Education and Personal Development

The effects of substance use extend into the educational and developmental realms, particularly harming children and adolescents.

- Disrupted Schooling: Children in households affected by addiction are more likely to struggle academically due to chronic stress, absenteeism, or lack of parental support.
- Developmental Delays: Exposure to a chaotic home environment can impede the emotional and cognitive growth of young children, affecting language acquisition, social skills, and self-esteem.
- Role Reversal and Parentification: Older children may be forced to assume adult responsibilities, caring for siblings or managing household affairs, which can stunt their own development and aspirations. These patterns can engender cycles of underachievement and lost potential, undermining the family's collective progress.

Physical Health and Safety Risks

Addiction brings with it a host of physical health complications—not only for the user, but for those around them.

- Neglect of Health and Hygiene: Substance use can lead to the neglect of basic health needs, including nutrition, sleep, and medical care.

- Exposure to Violence and Abuse: The chaos of addiction may result in physical neglect, child abuse, or domestic violence.
- Accidental Injuries and Fatalities: Intoxication increases the likelihood of accidents, injuries, and even death within the home.
- The household environment may become hazardous, stripping family members of their sense of safety and undermining physical well-being.

Social Isolation and Loss of Community

Families affected by substances frequently experience isolation, as stigma and shame discourage them from seeking support.

- Withdrawal from Social Networks: Fear of judgment may cause families to retreat from friends, neighbors, and extended family.
- Barriers to Support Services: Stigma can act as a barrier to accessing mental health care, family counseling, and addiction treatment.
- Intergenerational Transmission of Risk: Children raised in environments marked by addiction are more likely to struggle with social integration and may be at higher risk of substance use themselves.
- Isolation not only diminishes the immediate family's quality of life but also reduces their capacity to benefit from broader community resources and opportunities.

Legal and Ethical Consequences

Substance use may embroil families in legal trouble, further impeding their progress.

- Criminal Justice Involvement: Illegal drug use, driving under the influence, or substance-related violence can result in arrests, court proceedings, and incarceration.
- Loss of Custodial Rights: Parents struggling with addiction may lose custody of their children, causing long-term disruption and trauma.

- Ethical Dilemmas: Family members may resort to morally questionable actions—such as theft or fraud—to sustain an addiction or protect a loved one.

Legal challenges compound the difficulties families face, reinforcing cycles of instability and limiting their options for recovery.

Barriers to Recovery and Family Healing

While recovery is possible, substance use presents formidable obstacles that must be overcome for families to heal and progress.

- Denial and Resistance: Denial of the severity of the problem can stall intervention and prolong suffering.
- Fragmented Support Systems: Families may lack access to coordinated care, including addiction treatment, mental health services, and financial counseling.
- Relapses and Recurrence: The chronic nature of addiction means recovery is often a long, nonlinear process, fraught with setbacks that can test a family's resilience.
- Despite these barriers, hope remains. Families can and do recover, given the right resources, empathy, and support—but the journey requires time, commitment, and the willingness to confront painful truths.

Promoting Progress: Strategies for Resilience and Recovery

Families confronting substance use are not without recourse. There are tangible steps that can foster resilience and pave the way for progress.

- Seeking Professional Help: Engaging with therapists, addiction specialists, and support groups can provide crucial guidance and tools for recovery.
- Building Open Communication: Encouraging honest dialogue about substance use and its effects helps reduce shame and foster understanding.

- Strengthening Protective Factors: Focusing on education, employment, and healthy relationships can mitigate risks and support healing.
- Community Engagement: Connecting with community organizations and social services expands the family's network of resources and support.

Each family's journey is unique, but the capacity for renewal is universal. By acknowledging the dangers posed by substance use and taking proactive steps, families can reclaim their momentum, nurture each member's potential, and lay the groundwork for lasting progress.

Conclusion

The dangerous effects of substance use run far deeper than the individual, they ensnare entire families, jeopardizing emotional well-being, financial security, personal development, and the promise of a better future. Addressing the problem requires courage, compassion, and concerted effort from all corners of society. Only then can families break free from the cycle of addiction and restore the progress that is their birthright.

CHAPTER 7

VIOLENCE AGAINST WOMEN

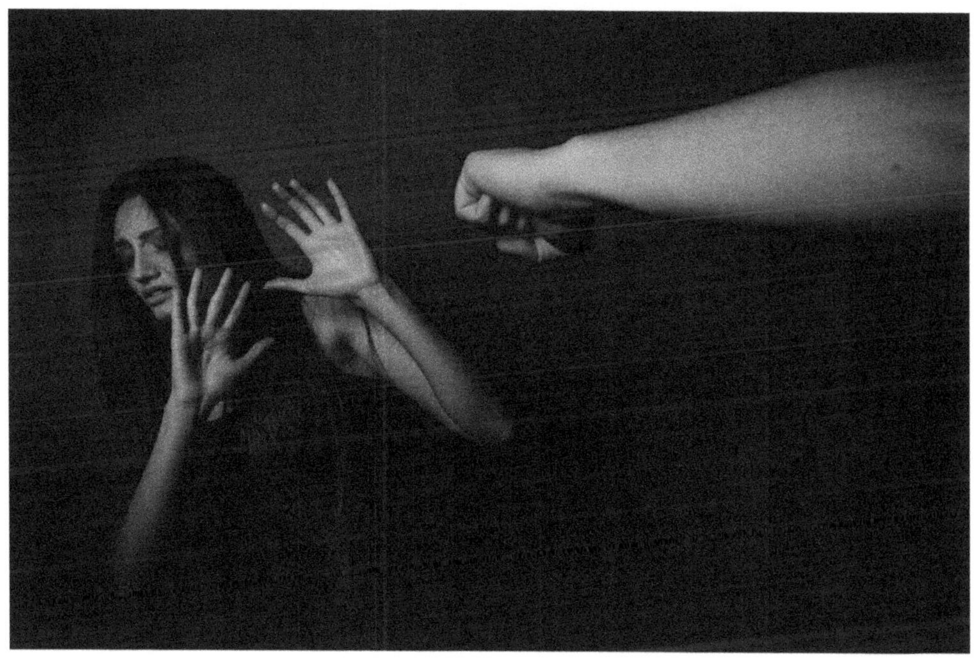

Introduction

Domestic violence is the willful intimidation, physical assault, battery, sexual assault and or other abusive behavior as part of perpetrated by one intimate partner against another. It includes physical violence, sexual violence, physical violence, and emotional abuse. Violence manifests within the family, in the home or in interpersonal relationships, and is inclusive of abuse, rape and sexual abuse. It also covers violence in the community, including rape, sexual abuse, torture, trafficking and forced prostitution, kidnapping and sexual harassment in workplace, in educational and health care institutions and other settings. Violence exercised by people or private institutions is also a violation of international law.

Violence against women takes many forms, from physical attacks to mental assault, including verbal abuse, extreme possessiveness or harassment. Physical attacks are often accompanied by sexual violence. A recent UN survey found that in countries as diverse as Kuwait, Samoa, Uganda, Chile, Poland and the US, violence against women is greatly exacerbated by alcohol and drug abuse. Most women are targets of violence in their role as wife or lover, but they are also victims as daughters, daughter-in-law, sisters, sisters-in-law, ex-wives, ex-lovers and mothers.

Since the frequency and intensity of attacks usually escalates with time, the longer a woman is victimized, the more likely she is to be seriously hurt or killed. Crime statistics from Canada show that 60% of all women murdered between 1961 and 1974 were killed within the family. Research from Thailand, Kenya, Bangladesh and Australia shows similar results, (The troubled Family by Boyden pp.99) Many criminologists believe that domestic violence against women is the most underreported crime. In incest cases especially, victims tend to feel humiliated and shamed, and sometimes guilty. Usually, they choose to put up with abuse rather than risk family breakup or social ostracism. Even when women and children do speak up, few people are prepared to listen or take them seriously. (Boyden, pp. 99) It is necessary to recognize that gender-based violence violates women's fundamental rights, which include the right to life, liberty and protection from discrimination and gender inequality as well as freedom of thought and the right not to be tortured.

Gender-based violence is understood as an obstacle to the full realization of women's potential and an impediment to their total participation in every sphere of life. As indicated in the Program of Action from the International Conference on Population and Development (Cairo, 1994) and the Beijing Conference (1995), gender-based violence is harmful to reproductive health. The convention is also applicable to that practice by institutions and health services that do not respect women's physical, social and moral integrity. To this end, medical treatment and experimentation are prohibited without the woman's consent. Respect for her body and her decisions are the foundation for the elimination of violence.

DOMESTIC VIOLENCE

Domestic violence is when one person does a variety of things to control another in an intimate relationship. Most people wonder if what is happening to them is domestic violence because their partner has never hit them. Physical abuse is probably what most people think of when they think about domestic violence, but it is just one of the many ways that your partner might try to gain power and control in your relationship.

This is a woman's nightmare. African women honor and obey their husbands, hold them in high esteem because it's inculcated in them from childhood, but men have turned it to dishonor and constant beatings. A 1997 study found that domestic violence is common in all regions and spans, all social classes and groups in the country, it results in significant physical, psychological and social impairment of women. The crisis of domestic violence is intensified by social and legal constructions of the family as "private" and popular perceptions of male power as normative.

This fuels the universal ideology of male supremacy that bestows on men the obligation and prerogative to chastise their wives. Regardless of social beliefs and ideologies about gender and family relations, the prospect of prohibiting and punishing domestic violence depends, foremost, on the state's willingness and capacity to reform criminal and family laws.

Though the Nigerian constitution guarantees equal rights to all citizens, including clauses that bar discrimination based on sex, it is still not enough to deter domestic violence. At the Nigerian National Assembly, a draft bill on domestic violence was not too long ago introduced, but it is inadequate because it merely addresses violence against women and not domestic violence. For what it is worth, maybe they should bring criminal law to bear on some aspects of intra-family violence and establish prohibitions and punishments for violence between family members.

SEXUAL VIOLENCE

A husband's sexual violence is generally a taboo topic, and so women victims feel anguished, fearful and ashamed of admitting it. A woman may be able to admit to being beaten, but to acknowledge that the man also forces her to have sex may cause her so much pain that it becomes the most difficult trauma to admit. This also includes making you engage in sexual acts that make you uncomfortable, forcing you to engage in prostitution.

PSYCHOLOGICAL VIOLENCE

Psychological violence provokes serious deterioration of the affected person's mental health, sometimes driving them to suicide. The higher rate of suicide does not appear to be related to a violent situation, but the links may become clear when the case is further investigated. A husband can destroy his wife psychologically, leave her isolated, prevent her from working, refuse to give her money and discredit her, calling her names, putting her down or embarrassing her in front of other people, criticizing your abilities as a partner or parent. In such cases, physical violence becomes superfluous.

Women seek medical treatment because of the anxiety violence provokes, and they are given tranquilizers. Then, when the husband comes home, they take the pills so as not to 'provoke' him. Medication makes them more vulnerable, and they are less able to escape from a violent situation. The experience of constant fear has a tremendous impact. It brings on emotional and psychological instability. A person who lives in expectation and fear of severe physical or psychological harm is incapable of visualizing himself in an alternative scenario.

Abused women generally visit medical Doctors because of their physical symptoms, because they are anxious or because they themselves are more violent with the children. A woman can be in therapy for years without ever stating that her real problem is violent. That is why it is so important to educate health professionals about this issue. It is also necessary to train the professionals responsible for initial treatment. They need to overcome the myths which make it difficult to perceive women's real needs. They must examine their own experiences with violence, their own family histories and ask themselves why they fail to consider certain types of behavior as violent.

PHYSICAL VIOLENCE

Battered women experience a variety of physical problems which could indicate that they are living in a violent situation. The physical symptoms are similar to those who live through prolonged periods of stress. The constant threat of life generates a level of stress sometimes impossible to bear. Physical violence includes pushing, grabbing, hitting, slapping, punching, or kicking you.

MINIMIZING, DENYING, BLAMING

This is done by making you think the abuse is your fault; saying the abuse was caused by stress, alcohol, or problems at work; it's your parent's fault to divide his family; he was spiritually attacked by his anniversaries against his marriage; denying that the abuse happened at all.

USING CHILDREN

This includes undermining your authority with your children; threatening to take the children away from you by kidnapping or getting custody of them; "pumping" your children for information about you to change, hate you and love him.

COERCION AND THREAT

This includes showing you a weapon and threatening to use it on you; threatening to paste your naked/ nude pictures on Facebook; threatening to harm your family, friends, or anyone you might go to for help.

LONELY SINGLE LADY

ISOLATION

It includes making it hard for you to see your friends and family; telling you that your friends and family cause problems in the relationship or are trying to" come between you"; cutting you off from people that care about you, your uncles, aunties, relations.

WORDS OF ENCOURAGEMENT/COMFORT TO DOMESTIC VIOLENCE SURVIVORS DELIVERED BY BEATRICE NWALOZIE ON OCTOBER 2014 ANNIVERSARY, AT BARRIER FREE LIVING, MANHATTAN, NEW YORK.

Learn to turn your pain into purpose, your messes into your message and your hurt into hope. Find peace and purpose in the hurts of your past. Using what you've gone through to minister to someone, that is true freedom. Your wounds need to heal and become scars. Don't revenge: Revenge means you are fighting your own battle and God becomes a spectator in your battlefield. No, let God fight it. Let go, hand over your pain, hurting, cries and all your loneliness over to Him and have your peace. God sees, knows, understands and will handle them all, victory and peace would be yours at last.

Refuse to lose hope at all as you journey through life. Determination and Hope are your passports to success. You need to be alive to see your dream come through, stop that worrying, bitterness and move on. Strive to cultivate the cheerful, hopeful disposition that will enable you to see the silver lining to every dark cloud. Let the abuser see and hear of your progress/success. Never pity yourself, your background, age or your level of education, move further from where you stopped. Keep HOPE ALIVE. Hope is the great echo of the spirit in us. All that you hope for by the grace of Almighty God, you shall have them.

No matter what challenges you face today, take comfort that the Almighty God knows every issue on your heart and is able to shoulder your burdens. Hold fast to the faithful one. Your challenges do not fall outside the scope of God's ability to intervene. God is mysterious, He's powerful and will see you through. When you lift your eyes from your situation and fix them on your Savior—when you choose to trust Him—you will find peace in pain and strength in the struggle. (Excerpt from Girlfriends in God)

My motto: This too shall pass. Today's Tips:

- Seeking out positive relationships and maintaining distance from individuals who exhibit negativity.
- Always be honest.
- Improve the world with your actions.
- Spend 7 minutes daily in quiet time with God.
- Stop the blame game and move on.
- Don't be lazy, find something to do.
- Exercise daily, it helps.
- Do what makes you happy.
- When no one else believes in your vision, keep it up, have the courage to on and be resourceful.
- Change is hard at the beginning, messy in the middle and gorgeous a end. Change comes with progress.
- Delete victim speeches from your vocabulary, like: "No more, I can't make it. It's not possible." "Why me?" "It's so bad and hard." Rather say: "I will make it." "This is awesome, fabulous, and great." "What's the opportunity?" and etc.
- Inspire someone today.
- Living in the past disrespects your future.
- Smile at people when you see them, say, please respect them and appreciate them.
- Be focus, goal setting, no procrastination.
- Remember that your greatest gift is so much stronger than your deepest (Excerpt from inspiration independent awakening).

LONELINESS IN SINGLE MOTHERS AND THEIR CHILDREN

An Exploration of Emotional, Psychological, and Social Consequences

Introduction

Being a single mother is an experience marked by both profound love and unique challenges. While single mothers often demonstrate remarkable resilience and resourcefulness, the weight of raising children alone can lead to episodes of acute loneliness. This sense of isolation does not exist in a vacuum; it can deeply affect both the mother and her children, shaping their emotional landscapes, mental health, and overall well-being.

Understanding Loneliness in Single Mothers Loneliness is a complex, multidimensional emotion, characterized not merely by being alone, but by feeling disconnected or unsupported. For single mothers, loneliness can result from the absence of a co-parent, limited social support, financial struggles, and the relentless demands of solo parenting. Unlike temporary bouts of solitude, chronic loneliness can become a persistent presence in a single mother's life, sometimes intensifying during major milestones, crises, or even everyday routines.

THE EFFECTS OF LONELINESS ON SINGLE MOTHERS

Emotional and Psychological Impact

Single mothers often carry the emotional labor of an entire household. Loneliness can amplify feelings of stress, anxiety, and depression. Without a partner to share responsibilities or offer emotional support, the weight of decision-making and problem-solving can become overwhelming. Over time, this emotional burden may manifest as:

- Depression and Anxiety: Persistent loneliness is strongly linked to depression and anxiety. Single mothers may feel a deep sense of sadness, hopelessness, or constant worry about their ability to provide for and support their children.

- Low Self-Esteem: The absence of affirmation from a partner or supportive network can erode a mother's confidence in her parenting and personal worth.
- Chronic Stress: Facing daily challenges alone can lead to chronic stress, which has well-documented effects on both mental and physical health.
- Burnout: The combination of emotional exhaustion, lack of respite, and feelings of isolation can result in parental burnout, characterized by irritability, fatigue, and emotional detachment.

Physical Health Consequences

The psychological strain of loneliness often manifests in the body, potentially leading to:

- Sleep Disturbances: Anxiety and overthinking can disrupt sleep patterns, leading to insomnia or poor-quality rest.
- Weakened Immune System: Chronic stress and loneliness can impair immune function, making single mothers more susceptible to illness.
- Somatic Complaints: Headaches, muscle tension, and gastrointestinal issues are common among those experiencing ongoing emotional strain.

Impact on Daily Functioning and Social Life

Loneliness may discourage single mothers from seeking out social interactions, either due to lack of time, feelings of inadequacy, or fear of judgment. This withdrawal can shrink their support network even further, creating a cycle of isolation. Practical obstacles, such as limited childcare or financial constraints, can exacerbate this pattern.

- Reduced Social Engagement: Single mothers might attend fewer community events, gatherings, or parent-teacher meetings, further limiting their connections.
- Difficulty Asking for Help: Loneliness can make it harder to reach out, perpetuating a sense of isolation and self-reliance.

THE IMPACT OF MATERNAL LONELINESS ON CHILD DEVELOPMENT

Children are keen observers, and the emotional climate of their home profoundly impacts their development. When a single mother experiences loneliness, the ripple effects can be felt by her children in several domains:

Emotional Development

Children may sense their mother's sadness or anxiety, even if not overtly expressed. This can lead to:

- Increased Anxiety or Insecurity: Children may become anxious about their mother's well-being or their family's stability.
- Emotional Withdrawal: Some children respond by becoming more withdrawn or self-reliant, while others may act out to seek attention or reassurance.
- Empathy and Role Reversal: In some cases, children take on a caregiving role for their mother, suppressing their own needs to provide comfort, which can impact their own emotional maturity and lead to "parentification."

Behavioral and Academic Impact

Loneliness in a single mother can translate into less emotional availability at home, affecting children's behavior and performance:

- Behavioral Challenges: Children may display increased irritability, aggression, or difficulty managing emotions.
- Academic Difficulties: Emotional distress at home can hinder concentration, motivation, and academic performance.
- Social Withdrawal: Children might mirror their mother's social withdrawal, participating less in extracurricular activities or peer interactions.

Social Skills and Relationships

Children learn social skills by observing and interacting with adults. When their primary caregiver is lonely or socially isolated, children may experience:

- Difficulty Forming Friendships: Children may struggle with trust or social engagement, mirroring their mother's hesitancy.
- Risk of Loneliness: The isolation experienced by the mother can become intergenerational, increasing the likelihood that children themselves experience loneliness.

Breaking the Cycle: Coping Strategies for Single Mothers

While loneliness can be pervasive, it is not insurmountable. There are strategies and resources that can help mitigate its effects for both mothers and children:

- Seeking Support Networks: Engaging with other parents, community groups, or online forums can provide emotional support and practical advice.
- Professional Help: Counseling or therapy offers a safe space to process emotions, develop coping mechanisms, and address depression or anxiety.
- Building Routine and Self-Care: Prioritizing self-care, even in small ways, can improve well-being and resilience.
- Encouraging Open Communication: Creating a home environment where feelings are discussed openly helps children process emotions and feel valued.
- Accessing Social Services: Many communities offer resources for single parents, including childcare assistance, financial aid, and educational opportunities.

Conclusion

The effects of loneliness as a single mother go beyond the individual; they ripple through family dynamics, affecting both the mother's well-being and her children's development. Addressing loneliness requires recognizing its impact, destigmatizing the need for help, and building bridges to support and community. Through understanding, empathy, and practical strategies, single mothers and their children can foster resilience, connection, and hope for a brighter future.

CHAPTER 8

SINGLE MOTHER AS PRIMARY BREADWINNERS

This chapter explores the prevalence of female headships and some of its demographic characteristics. A man's relationship as a husband does not define who you are as a person, this means, you need to study yourself and live a satisfactory and fulfilling life that always makes you happy. Today, between one-quarter and one third of all households are headed by single parents. Lone parenthood has always been a part of family life. In the past, early death in adulthood was one of its main causes. It could also be caused by frequent wars or epidemics; many were widows three or four times.

Today, high rates of separation and divorce, migration and births to women without partners are the major causes of single-parent families. Most people are driven into single parenthood, but for many it is only a temporary arrangement until they remarry. Life is difficult for single parents, especially single mothers, not least because of prejudice and social stigma. The sheer physical and emotional fatigue of raising children alone and trying to be the main source of both affection and authority at the same time, drains morale.

Lone teenage mothers are more vulnerable because early childbearing can cause health complications, poverty and social rejection. Lone fathers fare better than lone mothers because friends, relatives and neighbors are more likely to rally around to help. Research has shown that nine out of every ten lone parents are women. Men can move more freely in and out of parenting relationships than women; they can decline involvement in the maintenance, nurture, and upbringing of their children. In many cultures, male partners are often transient members of the household.

In wealthier parts of the world, some economically independent women are now choosing parenthood without a partner. To these women, single parenthood presents new challenges and new opportunities. In Africa and in Nigeria in particular, men drift to the cities in search of employment, leaving their young beautiful wives and children behind without any remorse. A few send remittances, but a good number do not. Compared to males, female householders are disadvantaged in many ways. They are more likely to be the head of the household due to circumstances, rather than choice. In the developing world, they married when young—their husbands were four to eight years older, on average—so they are less experienced in the ways of the world and less educated. It is far more difficult for women to maintain their families than men because they have less access to the market economy. When they do earn, their wages are generally far lower than men's.

BUSY SINGLE MOTHER

SOCIAL AND ECONOMIC FACTORS ASSOCIATED WITH THE EMERGENCE OF FEMALE HEADED HOUSEHOLDS

Most studies focus on the recent emergence of households maintained by females and their influence on the welfare of women and their children. Available evidence reveals that female headship was not uncommon in some cultures in the past. Having a woman as a household has been documented as a tradition in some African societies. For example, in Kwahu, a society in Ghana, a matrilineal descent group with a depth of about four generations is the most significant social group, with women running their daily subsistence. (Bleek, 1987)

Among the possible reasons for the recent increase in female headship is male migration, leaving women as household heads. During men's absence, by this instance women migrate in search of employment to take care of the children abandoned by the irresponsible man, women often become the household's heads in the place of destination. In countries of Eastern and Southern

Africa, young men were the first to accept wage employment on white-owned firms and mines, fostering male out-migration and a concomitant increase in female headship.

In the Caribbean, slavery stripped African men of authority over women and children. As a result, informed marriages became widespread in the region.

VULNERABILITY OF CHILDREN

Globally, many children take to living on the streets where they are persecuted and harassed by the police, shopkeepers, and local residents. These hungry and sick children are often drawn into drug and prostitution rings, the latter with the risk of unwanted pregnancies, backstreet abortion and infection from sexually transmitted diseases. They 'belong' to nobody, and children living without adults are easy prey—there is no one to defend them or to mourn their death, this is the plight of 'child-headed families' ; they are the most vulnerable family unit.

THE VULNERABILITY OF CHILDREN WHO ARE PRODUCTS OF DIVORCE

Understanding the Emotional, Social, and Developmental Consequences

Introduction

Divorce, once a subject shrouded in silence, is now a common feature of contemporary society. While adults navigate the complexities of separation, the true reverberations of divorce are often felt most acutely by children. These young witnesses and participants in the dissolution of family structures become, in many ways, the product of divorce—shaped by its emotional, social, and developmental currents. Their vulnerability, nuanced and multifaceted, demands empathetic exploration, both to understand its dimensions and to guide families and communities toward compassion and effective support.

Emotional Vulnerability

Children embroiled in the aftermath of divorce encounter a shifting emotional landscape, one marked by confusion, grief, and sometimes, lingering guilt. The disruption of a familiar home environment can provoke anxiety and sadness, as routines and relationships transform overnight. Younger children may struggle to articulate their feelings, expressing distress through changed behavior, becoming withdrawn, irritable, or regressing to earlier developmental stages.

Older children and adolescents, meanwhile, may experience acute feelings of loss or anger. They might direct blame inward, believing their actions contributed to parental discord, or outward, feeling betrayed by one or both parents. The emotional vulnerability of these children is further compounded by the sense of helplessness that accompanies witnessing adult conflict. The longing for stability and security becomes paramount, yet often elusive in the wake of divorce.

The Role of Parental Conflict

Research suggests that children's emotional well-being is more profoundly affected by parental conflict than divorce itself. Exposure to ongoing arguments, tension, or hostile communication can leave children feeling caught in the crossfire, torn by loyalty to both parents. This psychological strain may contribute to chronic stress, depression, and, in severe cases, trauma. Conversely, when parents manage to separate amicably, focus on co-parenting, and shield their children from conflict, the negative impact on children's emotional health can be markedly reduced.

Social Vulnerability

The social world of children is often inextricably linked to family stability. Divorce can disrupt friendships, routines, and even school performance. In cases where separation necessitates relocation, children must navigate new schools, communities, and peer groups, all while grappling with the emotional upheaval of family change.

Feelings of difference or isolation often emerge, particularly if divorce is less common among classmates. Children may become self-conscious about their family situation, reluctant to invite friends' home or speak openly about their experiences. Peer relationships can suffer, and the child may struggle to develop a sense of belonging in new social contexts.

Impact on Social Development

Social vulnerability may manifest as difficulties in trust, communication, and forming healthy relationships. Some children, wary of attachment after witnessing the dissolution of their parents' marriage, develop defenses against intimacy or conflict. Others may seek affirmation and stability from peers, sometimes engaging in risky behaviors or gravitating toward unhealthy relationships. The ability to adapt socially depends on a multitude of factors, including the child's temperament, parental support, and the broader community's acceptance and understanding.

Developmental Vulnerability

The disruptions occasioned by divorce extend into the developmental domain, potentially affecting academic achievement, behavioral regulation, and future aspirations. Studies have shown that children of divorce are at increased risk for academic challenges, including decreased grades, concentration difficulties, and diminished motivation. The emotional turmoil that accompanies divorce may sap the energy and focus required for learning, while changes in living arrangements can introduce logistical hurdles to consistent study and school attendance.

Developmentally, children may also experience challenges in identity formation and self-esteem. The reconfiguration of family roles and dynamics can prompt questions about loyalty, belonging, and self-worth. Adolescents may be thrust into premature responsibility, caring for younger siblings or acting as emotional mediators between parents. This "parentification" can accelerate maturity but may also burden young people with stress and anxiety ill-suited to their developmental stage.

Long-Term Consequences

The vulnerability engendered by divorce does not dissipate as children grow older; instead, it can shape their perspectives on relationships, commitment, and family. Some may become wary of long-term attachment, fearing repetition of their parents' experience. Others may become resilient, learning from their circumstances to forge strong, empathetic bonds in adulthood. The long-term impact is not predetermined but mediated by a host of factors—parental behavior, the presence of supportive adults, access to counseling, and the child's own coping mechanisms.

Protective Factors and Resilience

Not all children who experience divorce succumb to its vulnerabilities. Many emerge with remarkable resilience, navigating change with adaptability and strength. Protective factors play a crucial role in this process, buffering children from the worst effects and nurturing their ability to thrive.

Key among these are:

- Consistent, loving parenting: When parents remain engaged and supportive, children feel secure and valued, mitigating feelings of abandonment and loss.
- Open communication: Encouraging children to express their emotions, ask questions, and voice concerns helps prevent internalization of distress.
- Stable routines: Regular schedules and familiar rituals foster a sense of normalcy and predictability in children's lives.
- Access to counseling or support groups: Professional guidance provides tools for coping, understanding, and healing.
- Involvement of extended family and community: Grandparents, aunts, uncles, teachers, and mentors can offer additional layers of emotional and practical support.

Guidance for Parents and Caregivers

For parents facing divorce, the imperative is clear: prioritize the well-being of children above all else. This means minimizing exposure to conflict, avoiding negative talk about the other parent, and reassuring children of their unconditional love and support. Maintaining open channels of communication and involving children in decisions where appropriate fosters empowerment, rather than helplessness.

It is vital for caregivers to pay attention to warning signs of distress—changes in behavior, mood, or performance—and to seek professional help when needed. Creating opportunities for children to process their feelings, whether through play, art, or conversation, can facilitate healing.

Conclusion

The vulnerability of children who are products of divorce is real, profound, and deserving of thoughtful attention. While the impact of divorce can be challenging, it is not insurmountable. With understanding, support, and resilience-building strategies, children can navigate the tumult of family change and emerge with strength and hope. Society has a responsibility to recognize these vulnerabilities and to offer the resources and compassion necessary for every child to flourish—no matter the shape of their family.

MOTHER/CHILD CO-RESIDENCE, BY MOTHER'S MARITAL STATUS

The chances of a child living apart from the mother differ sharply according to the mother's marital status. Children are most likely to be living with mothers who are currently in their first marital union, regardless of the children's age. For very young children (Less than 5-18 years old), the divorced or separated group of mothers usually have the highest percentage living or residing with their mothers in developing countries.

Increasing urbanization and industrialization have caused a greater number of women to change the nature of their work and to seek cash-earning activities. Even if they are low paid or insecure, the increasing labor force participation of women is likely to increase the total household income and to affect its expenditures. A large fraction of women in developing countries are working mothers owing to the combination of economic pressure and relatively high fertility. When maternal employment means long hours away from home, with little help for childcare, an overall negative impact on children can be expected. Maternal work outside the home would reduce the mother's time available to spend with her children. Mother's work might affect infants' feeding practices and nutritional status of children, especially when the children are small. Children ensure their parents' acceptance within their families and communities.

Indeed, several studies have demonstrated that maternal employment can have a positive effect on a child's welfare. Women's paid job increases the overall family income, which benefits all family members, including young children (Tucker, 1989; United Nations, 1992). Other authors argue that more of women's income compared to men's income is spent on child-oriented expenses such as food, clothing and education.

CHAPTER 9

FAMILY MATTERS

The family constitutes one of various social relationships within society, each possessing distinct characteristics. This section examines the peculiarities of the family unit, focusing on how it links its members through social, legal, and economic connections, as well as through strong emotional bonds. The composition and nature of the family evolve over time, reflecting events such as the birth and upbringing of children, their progression to adulthood, and the ageing of its original members. Nevertheless, the family persistently serves as a dynamic link among individuals across generations.

The text discusses growing concerns about protecting individual rights and wellbeing, particularly for vulnerable family members. In families, each person's actions and health impact one another. Currently, the economic and social prospects of children from low-and middle-income families are being threatened by societal trends such as teenage sex, divorce, cohabitation, and childbirth outside of marriage. Mary E. Williams argues that poverty and inequality are deeply connected to whether or not marriage is present in society, noting that nearly half of American families fall into poverty after a divorce.

Three-fourths of women seeking welfare do so after a marriage disruption. Studies indicate that children of divorced or single parents are more likely to face academic challenges, health issues, and increased risk of addiction, crime, and poverty. Additionally, those whose parents split between ages five and sixteen are more prone to emotional and conduct disorders.

Research indicates that a child's family background is as influential as household health, income, and education. According to Stephen Lunn (News Corp Australia), children from broken homes often struggle with completing school and securing employment. These children are more likely to have multiple live-in relationships as adults, and girls from divorced families face increased rates of teenage motherhood. Additionally, children from divorced families tend to prefer de facto relationships over marriage to mitigate social and economic risks.

MEN AND WOMEN

Men and women all over the world need to belong to a home, and a family which is your identity where you can easily be located. The marital bond is not only expected to fulfill the needs of the individual. Society, too, benefits from it for thousands of years, marriage has provided an ideal opportunity to forge alliances between groups, as to secure the future with heirs. It is more than a bond between husband and wife.

Cousin marriage is a longstanding practice common in parts of Africa, such as Nigeria, and Asia. In some areas of Pakistan and India, up to half of all marriages are between cousins to preserve family wealth. In contrast, 30 US states ban cousin marriage, with eight considering it a criminal offense (Boyden, 1997).

WOMEN'S WORK AND MEN'S WORK

It's possible that gender inequality has not always existed. In prehistoric times, women were valued for their unique connection to nature: they gave birth and grew much of the food. These qualities were among the first human traits to be celebrated in religious traditions.

However, as women's roles shifted toward seeking white-collar employment, the importance of raising children, growing food, and maintaining the home declined. Since men generally dominated paid and mechanized work, official statistics sometimes misleadingly suggest that women are not working at all.

Women's significant contributions to family life and essential goods production are frequently overlooked. In many parts of Sub-Saharan Africa, women handle demanding agricultural work alongside childcare and household responsibilities. Despite perceptions of reduced gender inequality, data indicate women remain economically disadvantaged and often work more hours than men, both at home and in paid employment.

CHAPTER 10

MEN AND FATHERS

Demonstrating respect and consideration for your spouse serves as an important example for your children. Observing positive interactions, such as assisting with household responsibilities or expressing thoughtful gestures, can influence your children's perception of respectful relationships. Children notice how you treat their mother and others, and consistent displays of kindness and care can reinforce their expectations of healthy interpersonal dynamics. Establishing regular, respectful engagement with your spouse promotes a constructive environment that benefits the entire family.

Never derogate or talk down to your wife, especially in front of your kids. Instead build her up with praises on a constant basis. Don't be fooled, our children hear every word, and they notice how you treat one of their two most favorite people. A father must find a way to balance being both parent and friend to their kids. You must build genuine friendships with your kids if you are going to be approachable and have a lasting impact on their lives. Henry Ward Beecher, said: "There is no friendship, no love like that of the parents for the child."

Men's self-perceptions and expectations as husbands and fathers differ greatly both across and within cultures. Generally, many men do not have the authority to be loving and caring fathers and are physically absent from their children for a variety of reasons, such as separation, divorce, deliberate irresponsibility, or migration to cities or other countries in search of work/high pay and great living environment. Even when living in the same home, most men are absent from the process of rearing their young children.

As countries industrialize, the role of fathers in families becomes increasingly tied to work away from home; their role as a socializer of children declines. Studies tend to confirm the male tendency to identify more with the 'provider' role than the 'nurture?' role, and many feel inadequate in the "women's domain" of childcare and development. George Forman said "Fatherless homes are at epidemic proportions. As a result, there's a whole generation of kids who lack direction." But generally, children who grow up in a stable, two-parent family have the best prospects for achieving income security as adults. You must defend, protect, sacrifice, make unpopular decisions, take the pressure, and carry the load, while at the same time being loving, wise and understanding. Successful fatherhood seems an impossible task.

Well, the truth is, it is impossible without the help of the good Lord. God gives wisdom, knowledge and encouragement, when you neglect God, your family is in jeopardy.

PARENTING

Communicating with children

"We need to assure our children that their feelings are important to us. If they think otherwise, they will keep their concerns locked inside or turn elsewhere for help." – Maranda.

"Don't overreact, even if your child's thinking is way off center." – Anthony.

Take advantage of informal settings when they're ready to open up. Sometimes children open up when they are not sitting face-to-face with a parent. "We take advantage of car rides. Being side-by-side rather than across from each other has led to good discussions." – Nicole

Mealtime presents another opportunity for informal conversation.

"At dinnertime each of us relates the worst thing and the best thing that happened that day. This practice unites us and lets each of us know that we don't have to face problems alone." – Robin

DISCIPLINE

The word Discipline can mean to guide or to teach. At times, that includes correcting a child's misbehavior. Often, though, it involves imparting moral training that helps a child learn to make good choices in the first place. In recent decades, discipline has all but disappeared from some households, as parents fear that correction might lower a child's self-esteem. However, wise parents set reasonable rules and train their children to abide by them. "Children need boundaries to help them grow into well-rounded adults. Without discipline, children are like a rudderless ship, which will eventually go off course or even capsize. – Pamela

As Parents:

- Be Consistent. If your child does not adhere to your rules, enforce consequences. On the other hand, readily commend your child when he or she complies.
- "I frequently commend my children for their being obedient in a world where obedience is so rare. Commendation makes it easier for them to accept corrections when they are needed.' – Christiane

- Be Reasonable. Balance the child's age and competency level with the weight of the infraction. Consequences are usually most effective when they are related to the wrong, for example, misuse of a phone might result in loss of phone privileges for a period. At the same time, avoid making major issues over minor irritations.
- "I try to determine if my child has been deliberately disobedient or if he just made an error in judgment. There is a difference between a serious trait that needs to be weeded out and a mistake that just needs to be pointed out. – Wendell
- Be Loving. Discipline is much easier for children to accept and apply when they know that a parent's primary motive is love.
  "When our son made mistakes, we reassured him that we were proud of all the good decisions he had made in the past. We explained that the mistake wouldn't define him as long as made the needed correction and that we were there to help him do that." – Daniel

Discipline guides a child the way a rudder steers a boat and keeps it on course.

TRUSTWORTHY

Trustworthy people earn the confidence of their parents, friends and employers. They abide by the rules, keep their promises, and always tell the truth. Certainly, the amount of freedom you receive is directly related to the level of trust you have earned over time.

"The best way to earn your parents' trust is to demonstrate that you are mature and responsible, not only when you are with them but also when they are not around." – Sarahi

To earn more trust.

Be honest. Nothing will shatter others 'trust in you quicker than lies. Conversely, when you are open and honest—especially about your mistakes—you can earn the trust of others. "It's easy to be honest when things are going well, but being honest about things that cast you in a bad light goes a long way in building trust." – Caiman.

Be dependable. In the U.S. Survey, 78 percent of human-resource professionals indicate that reliability was "one of the three most important skills for entry-level positions". Learning to be dependable now will benefit you as an adult.

"My parents notice when I'm responsible and do my chores without their having to nag me. The more I show initiative like that, the more they reward it with their trust." – Sarah

Be patient. Unlike physical growth, which is readily apparent to others, time is often needed for others to recognize emotional and mental growth. "There's no single act that can earn the trust of your parents and others. But you can build it gradually if you're consistently responsible over time." – Brandon.

Goal setting – Goals are like blueprints; with effort, you can turn them into reality.

A goal is more than just a dream, something you wish would happen. Real goals involve planning, flexibility, and good, old-fashioned hard work. Goals can be short-range (taking days or weeks to accomplish), medium range (months), and long-range (a year or more). Long-range goals can be reached through a series of intermediate specific objectives.

Reaching goals can boost your confidence, strengthen your friendships and increase your happiness.

- Self-confidence: When you set small goals and reach them, you gain the confidence to take on bigger ones. You also feel more confident when facing day-to-day challenges such as standing up to peer pressure.
- Friendships: People enjoy being around those who are reasonably goal-oriented, that is, those who know what they want and are willing to work for it. Moreover, one of the best ways to strengthen a friendship is to work with another person toward a common goal.
- Happiness: When you set and reach goals, you feel a sense of accomplishment.

"I love having goals. They keep me occupied and give me something to keep reaching for. And when you reach a goal, it feels great to look back and say, 'Wow, I really did it! I accomplished what I set out to do.'" – Christopher. It's good to set a realistic goal and deadline, plan the steps involved, anticipate obstacles, and think of how to overcome them. Do not wait until you have every detail worked out to get started. Ask yourself, 'What is the very first thing I can do toward reaching my goal?' Track your progress as you complete each step with diligence.'

TIME FATHER SPENT WITH CHILDREN

A study of four-year olds in 10 countries discovered that the average daily time spent alone by fathers with their children was less than one hour, ranging from 6 minutes per day in Hong Kong and 12 minutes in Thailand to 50 minutes in China and 48 minutes in Finland. When the average time spent with both parents was added in, the number of hours fathers were present with their children ranged from 1 hour and 36 minutes in the US to 3 hours and 42 minutes in Belgium. These findings suggest that even though fathers are present as active members of a family, their direct involvement in childcare can be very limited.

The nineteenth century ideal of the father was a remote but authoritarian figure. Fathers did much work at home before the industrial revolution and the family often worked together as an economic unit. The industrial revolution greatly enhanced man's authority in the home. With increased earning power, a man's status was marked by ability to provide for his wife and children. If his wife was forced to work, he was thought to have failed as a man and as a husband. In most societies today, a man is expected by tradition and religion to' keep' his wife and children: to be the 'bread winner' and the head of the house. Fathers usually provide for the family and though they buy toys, they will rarely play with the children. They must learn that interaction with their children is important and necessary. Research suggests, however, that there is a connection between lack of a father figure and problems such as delinquency and low academic achievement in children.

The industrial work ethic is hostile to fatherhood. Men's devotion to work and absence from the home is deemed to be natural. Men are expected to put their work first; the role of the father is seen in relation to the workplace. Few companies plan for their male employees to become fathers or grant paid paternity leave. Concessions for mothers, such as childcare facilities at work, maternity leave are denied to fathers. Men and employers may need to re-evaluate their roles and responsibilities.

Media images of fatherhood have been undergoing a quiet revolution. In a study of the US media, it was found that the pre 1970 depiction of men as caregivers was of humbling, ineffective individuals. Today, this has changed to a potentially effective and important role in the social and emotional development of children. Also in the US, a magazine "Full-Time Dad" is published for care-giving fathers hoping to end the isolation that fathers who deeply care for their children often face. The joys and pleasures of nurturing children are key features of the magazine. Men who miss out on the nurturing role within a family miss some of the greatest joys in life.

FAMILY TURMOIL

Industrialization not only propelled men into higher status occupations; it also gave women paid employment. These days, many urban families cannot meet their material needs with a single income. Globally, women are becoming the majority sex in the workforce due to men's unemployment rate and job selection. Nowadays, the distribution of authority within the family is less clear than in the past.

Increasingly, men and women must negotiate the terms of their partnership. Husbands may choose to stay at home to care for children if their wives have greater earning power: Few couples have the courage to adopt this lifestyle in practice. In one U.S study, only 4 out of 3600 men cared for their children.

Parenthood is physically exhausting, requiring patience, endurance and commitment. It is also uniquely rewarding and challenging, changing the way adults live and think. Children are a source of great happiness, fascination, and pride, such as when they take their first steps or babble their first words. They have a dramatic impact on the status of marriage, too. Wedding toasts promise fertility and the personal fulfillment of having children.

BUILDING THE FAMILY

Both women and men should be given greater choice about how they balance their work and family lives. We all need to put our hands on deck to make sure that family institutions succeed for future generations, we have been beneficiaries, to the gains derived from living and coming out from a family. Modifying the organization of employment itself, both women and men may be given greater choice about how they balance their work and family lives. Employers can play their part by introducing flexible working schedules which include part time, job sharing, term-time and twilight shifts enabling parents and those with adult defendants to adjust work demands to home responsibly. Providing for career breaks such as maternity and paternity leave, without letting them jeopardize opportunities for promotion.

Emphasis can also be placed on assisting parents to re-enter the workforce by offering childcare in the workplace. Adapting the opening hours of service facilities such as health centers and childcare can benefit family welfare. The profit in using family-friendly measures far outweigh the cost-workers, attract a wider pool of applicants, reduce labor turnover and match lab. For women, family-friendly measures are viral. They improve access to and help to remove women's handicap in the job market, since they are the ones who work part-time or leave employment for several years to raise the family. Supportive employers can also provide positive options for men to help them create closer bonds with their children, and to force a climate of opinion in which men are seen as active parents sharing domestic responsibilities with women.

A family's income is used to finance immediate needs and, if it is sufficient, may allow the family to save for future needs. There are two elements in the amount of income received: the dollar value of hours worked, and the number of hours worked. These in turn are affected by, among other things, the parents' education level and work habits that typically are formed in the early years. The relationship between poverty and the absence of intact marriages is indeed very strong.

THE ESSENCE OF PARENTING AND THE DUTIES OF PARENTS

A Comprehensive Exploration of Parental Responsibilities

Parenting is one of the most profound human experiences, encompassing the nurturing, guidance, and support of a child from infancy through adulthood. It is both a privilege and a responsibility, demanding patience, empathy, dedication, and adaptability. Across cultures and eras, the meaning of parenting and the duties of parents have evolved, but the central aim remains the same: to foster the holistic development of children, enabling them to become responsible, compassionate, and capable individuals.

Understanding Parenting

At its core, parenting is about more than simply raising children—it is an ongoing process of teaching, modeling, protecting, and loving. It involves creating a safe and nurturing environment, instilling values, and preparing children to navigate the complexities of life.

Parenting is not limited to biological parents; it extends to adoptive parents, guardians, and any adult who assumes the vital role of caring for a child. The relationship between parent and child is foundational to the child's emotional security and overall well-being.

Effective parenting is characterized by:

- Unconditional love: Providing acceptance, warmth, and support regardless of circumstances.
- Guidance and discipline: Establishing boundaries, teaching right from wrong, and helping children develop self-control.
- Support and encouragement: Fostering self-esteem, confidence, and independence.
- Protection and safety: Ensuring the child's physical, emotional, and psychological well-being.
- Education and enrichment: Encouraging curiosity, learning, and growth through formal education and life experiences.

THE DUTIES OF PARENTS

Parenting duties are diverse and far-reaching. While each family's circumstances are unique, certain core responsibilities are common to all parents, regardless of their background, gender, or the specifics of their relationship.

Providing Basic Needs

Parents are responsible for meeting the basic needs of their children:

- Shelter: Ensuring a safe, stable, and comfortable living environment.
- Nutrition: Offering a balanced diet to support physical and cognitive development.
- Health care: Accessing appropriate medical care, vaccinations, and regular check-ups.
- Clothing: Supplying weather-appropriate attire that fits and is comfortable.

Emotional Support and Love

Children thrive in environments where they feel loved and valued. Parents must:

- Show affection through words and actions.
- Listen to their children's concerns, hopes, and feelings.
- Encourage self-expression and validate emotions.
- Help children develop coping skills for life's challenges.

Education and Intellectual Growth

Parents facilitate learning both within and outside the classroom by:

- Encouraging curiosity and a love of learning.
- Supporting academic achievement and lifelong learning.
- Providing opportunities for creative and critical thinking.
- Exposing children to cultural, artistic, and intellectual experiences.

Setting Boundaries and Discipline

Discipline is not about punishment, but about teaching children self-regulation, respect, and responsibility:

- Establishing consistent rules and consequences.
- Modeling respectful behavior and communication.
- Helping children understand the impact of their actions on others.
- Fostering a sense of accountability and integrity.

Fostering Independence

As children grow, parents gradually grant more autonomy:

- Encouraging children to make appropriate age decisions.
- Allowing them to learn from mistakes and successes.
- Supporting the development of practical life skills.
- Preparing children to manage responsibilities independently.

Protecting from Harm

Safety is paramount. Parents must:

- Monitor and supervise children to prevent accidents and abuse.
- Teach children about personal safety, boundaries, and risk awareness.
- Create secure environments at home, school, and in the community.
- Advocate for their children's welfare in all spheres of life.

Instilling Values and Ethics

Parents play a crucial role in shaping their children's character:

- Modeling honesty, kindness, empathy, and respect.
- Discussing ethical dilemmas and choices.
- Encouraging social responsibility and civic engagement.
- Fostering tolerance and appreciation for diversity.

The Collaborative Duties of Both Parents

In families with two parents, whether wife and husband or any other combination, shared responsibilities and mutual support are essential. Both partners contribute their unique strengths, perspectives, and resources to the well-being of their children.

Shared Responsibilities

- Cooperating in decision-making: Discussing and agreeing on major decisions regarding health, education, discipline, and family values.
- Balancing work and family life: Coordinating schedules and responsibilities to ensure quality time with children.
- Supporting each other emotionally: Encouraging open communication, empathy, and teamwork.
- Presenting a united front: Consistency in rules and expectations from both parents helps children feel secure.
- Dividing household and child-rearing tasks: Sharing chores, errands, and caregiving duties according to strengths, availability, and agreements.

Role Modeling

Both parents serve as role models:

- Demonstrating respectful relationships and problem-solving.
- Modeling healthy communication and conflict resolution.
- Showing children how to balance personal ambitions with family responsibilities.

Nurturing Individual Relationships

Each parent builds a unique bond with their children:

- Spending individual time with each child to foster trust and understanding.
- Celebrating achievements, milestones, and personal growth.
- Recognizing and responding to the distinct needs and personalities of each child.

Adapting to Change

Family life is dynamic. Both parents are responsible for:

- Adjusting parenting strategies as children grow and circumstances evolve.
- Supporting each other during life transitions, such as moving, career changes, or health challenges.
- Seeking help and guidance when needed, whether from family, friends, or professionals.

Challenges and Growth

Parenting is rewarding but not without challenges. There are times of doubt, fatigue, and frustration. However, these moments offer opportunities for growth, learning, and deeper connection within the family.

Parents are not expected to be perfect. Instead, they are called to be present, responsive, and willing to learn. Seeking support from each other, extended family, and the community can greatly enhance parenting journey.

Conclusion

Parenting is a lifelong commitment shaped by love, responsibility, and the unending desire to see children flourish. The duties of parents, whether as individuals or partners—are vast and varied, encompassing every aspect of a child's development. Through cooperation, understanding, and shared purpose, parents can create a nurturing environment that empowers children to reach their fullest potential and contribute positively to the world.

In summary, parenting is about being a guide, protector, and supporter. It is an act of devotion and partnership, where both parents—regardless of gender or role—work together to raise confident, kind, and capable individuals, ready to face life's adventures and challenges with courage and wisdom.

25 qualities of husbands who love their wives by Author Dr. Robert Lewis:

1. Includes his wife in envisioning the future.
2. Accepts spiritual responsibility for his family.
3. He is willing to say, "I'm sorry" and "Forgive me" to his family.
4. Discusses household responsibilities with his wife and makes sure they distribute.
5. Seeks consultation from his wife on all major financing decisions.
6. Follows through with commitments he has made to his wife.
7. Anticipates the different stages his children will pass through.
8. Anticipates the different stages his marriage will pass through.
9. Frequently he tells his wife what he likes about her.
10. Provides financially for his family's basic living expenses.
11. Deals with distraction so he can talk with his wife and family.
12. Prays with his wife on a regular basis.

13. Initiates meaningful family traditions.
14. Initiate fun family outings for the family on a regular basis.
15. Takes the time to give his children practical instructions about life.
16. Manages the schedule of the home and anticipates pressure points.
17. Keeps his family financially sound and out of harmful debt.
18. Make sure he and his wife have drawn up a will.
19. Let's his wife and children into the interior of his life.
20. Honors his wife in public.
21. Explains sex to each child in a way that gives them a wholesome perspective.
22. Encourages his wife to grow as an individual.
23. Take the lead in establishing sound family values.
24. Provides time for his wife to pursue her own personal interests.
25. Is involved in a small group of men dedicated to spiritual growth.

The marriage of the parents has much to do with a child's educational attainment and work ethic. The relationship can be expressed as an equation: Income = (education attained) x (work ethic) x) unity of family structure). Of course, one does not obtain an adequate and steady income just by marrying. Increasing the number of hours worked at a job valued by the marketplace will provide more income.

The number of hours worked is linked directly to educational achievement and family structure. Families whose members have lower levels of education will have to work longer to reach a modest level of financial security than those whose members achieve higher levels of education. Although the income of a family household depends on the educational level of parents, it is the parents' income rather than their level of education that predicts more accurately the level of education their children will achieve.

In general, children with high-income parents receive more education than children of lower income parents. Education gives the child from a high-income family a great advantage. Today, social science research broadly characterizes the children who are most likely to attain a good income as adults: They have parents who are married; they finish school, get a job, abstain from intercourse until marriage, and marry before having children of their own. But family structure plays an even larger role in children's future prosperity than those who have formulated public policy over the past 30 years have been willing to admit. Having a baby out of wedlock usually derails progress toward achieving a stable family structure and income.

It is not that the number of babies born to teens has changed; it is that marriage within this group has vanished. In addition, almost half of the mothers of out-of-wedlock children will go on to have another child out of wedlock. More than any other group, teenage mothers who give birth outside of marriage spend more of their lives as single parents. Not surprisingly, their children spend more time in poverty than do children of any other family structure. A single-parent family background and the poverty that usually accompanies it make children twice as likely to drop out of high school.

United Family

CHAPTER 11

THE SILENT STRUGGLE OF LOVE

Meaningful examples of family life that resonate with both married and unmarried individuals are reflected in my narrative.

What is marriage without hope?

It is a state marked by emotional emptiness, lack of connection, and little hope for improvement. Partners may co-exist without passion or intimacy, often holding resentment or blame due to unresolved issues or crises like infidelity or addiction. When effort stops and change seems impossible, the relationship decays—even if the couple stays together. It feels like:

- A sense of being stuck in a cycle.
- Overwhelming and exhausting.
- Dread or apathy towards the partner.

Bringing HOPE back.

- Have a regular date with your spouse
- Do monthly budget meetings to review and plan financial concerns and needs,
- Attend yearly or bi-yearly enrichments activities like counseling, retreats etc.
- Do something together that you both are passionate about.
- Be honest with your spouse and tell yourselves what you admire in one another,
- Practice non-sexual touch without it leading to sex,
- Do not blame your spouse on anything, own your actions,
- Do not use the word divorce unless you are filing it.
- Do not let your life become consumed with work, substance use, social media, video games, food or TV,
- Do not hide behind your kids' activities to avoid conflicts
- Do not use your kids to fulfill your loneliness. By Samuel Rainey.

Moments of resilience

One notable demonstration of my resilience was securing a contract with UNESCO to promote the concept of girls' education in Northern Nigeria, including examining both the advantages and challenges associated with educating girls.

Girl Child education is crucial for empowerment, economic growth, and better health outcomes, reducing poverty, child marriage and mortality rates.

Challenges like poverty, cultural norms, gender inequality, early marriages, poverty, distance between home and school violence, and lack of resources hinder it, while advantages include increased lifetime earnings, improved family health, greater community participation and breaking cycles of disadvantages for future generations.

When I heard this news, I was elated, happy and back to myself. I busted with pride, I was over the moon, excited. He comes to the house to pick up the kids from school, giving me more time to work on my research.

Healing language of tears

Ibitoru was always crying whenever she had issues with her spouse. Ogechi would send her brother's wife to always check up on *Ibitoru*. So, does crying solve problems? asked Ogechi. Crying does not directly solve problems, but it has a medicinal way of easing out the problem. It is a healthy emotional release that helps you process them by reducing stress hormones, releasing endorphins, self-soothing through the parasympathetic nervous system, and fostering social connection, leading to a clearer head to tackle issues afterwards. It does not offer immediate solutions, crying can improve mood, facilitate grief, and create vulnerability that strengthen bonds, making you more resilient and ready to find solutions through other means like talking or problem solving.

Benefits of crying include:

Stress reduction, mood regulation, self-soothing, emotional processing and social bonding.

Choosing wisdom while seeking answers

Getting advice or information from people that have experienced what you are passing through could help. *Ngozi* was concerned with seeking advice from Obinna. *Emeka* directed *Ngozi* to start visiting the libraries to read good books on family and marriage issues. Amazing books to read instead of seeking advice from friends and relatives that might not know much about her condition. This made *Ngozi* reduce the spread of her marital problems, then concentrated on going to the libraries daily.

Finding calm in peaceful places

- Adaugo enjoys activities like sightseeing, visiting museums, and watching sports to take her mind off marital issues. Museum visits can reduce stress, foster positive emotions, and provide couples with opportunities to bond over shared interests, ultimately improving relationships.
- Studies show that museums help lower cortisol and promote calm, making them a low-pressure environment for couples.

When action speaks louder than words

My friend *Chukwudalu* explained that he loves his wife and that his wife loved him as much, but he travelled outside his country and started messing around with girls. He said that he thought he was exploring life with his boyfriend *Osita* who also had his own girlfriend. When he went back home for a few weeks to see his wife and children. He tried making love to his wife, his dick was no more working. He wanted to make love to his wife *Njideka* but was surprised he could not. *Njideka* tried helping him by putting up a pornographic video, but to no avail. He hugged *Njideka* saying that he was sorry. *Njideka* asked him why he was sorry, what happened? Many questions but no response. *Chukwuemeka* could not explain to her what happened and the type of life he was living over there. Apparently, he forgot he is a married man.

What should be the way forward? Yes, betrayal causes hurt, anger and confusion. Infidelity, cheating on the innocent wife. These feelings are valid. Do not minimize them to keep peace.

Ask yourself: Can I continue in this marriage if this behavior continues? What must be changed for me to stay?

Decide your boundaries. Boundaries are about what you will accept, not controlling him. Do not blame yourself. His decision to cheat is his responsibility, not a failure on your part.

For the couple

Have an honest, direct conversation. The husband must take responsibility without excuses (distance, loneliness, culture, alcohol, etc.)

This requires accountability. If reconciliation is considered, it should include:

- Complete honesty
- Ending all outside relationships
- Transparency (travel behavior, communication)
- Willingness to rebuild trust over time.

Seeking counseling

A neutral third party (marriage counselor or therapist) is strongly recommended, especially with long-distance or travel-based marriages.

Allow time - don't rush forgiveness

Forgiveness is a process, not a demand. Healing takes consistency, not promises.

If he refuses to change

- The wife should prioritize self-respect, emotional well-being, and safety.
- Separation may be necessary if boundaries are ignored or trust cannot be rebuilt.
- Staying in a marriage where disrespect continues can cause long-term emotional harm.
- Love without respect is not enough to sustain a marriage.
- Change is shown through actions, not apologies.

Respect begins with responsibility

Ijeoma developed an infection after sleeping with her boyfriend, *Obinna*. When she told him about her symptoms, *Obinna* claimed he was fine. As *Ijeoma's* pain worsened, she visited her doctor for testing. The test confirmed she has a vaginal infection. The doctor advised her boyfriend to get tested as well so both can receive treatment and further guidance.

Ijeoma spoke to her boyfriend, *Obinna,* about the issue. He was upset and refused to go. She pleaded with him, but he still declined. What are her options?

In this situation, the woman should prioritize her health, safety and self-respect.

- Put her health first immediately.
- Complete all medical tests and treatment exactly as prescribed by the doctor.
- Avoid sexual contact until treatment is finished and a doctor confirms it's safe.
- She should clearly tell him that he must get tested and treated.
- Refusing to see a doctor puts her health at risk.
- This is not about blame, it is responsibility, integrity, honesty.
- If he continues to refuse getting tested and treatment, this is a RED FLAG.

A partner who refuses testing may be:

- Hiding something.
- Unconcerned about her health.
- Avoiding responsibility.
- Putting his comfort above her safety.
- This behavior shows lack of care and respect.

If he continues to refuse medical care:

Protect herself going forward

- Do not resume intimacy unless he provides proof of testing and treatment.
- Use protection if she chooses to continue the relationship (though trust is already damaged).

- Be willing to walk away if necessary. Staying exposes her to repeat infections, long-term health issues, and emotional harm.

The truth is that someone who truly loves you will not gamble with your health. Refusing testing after causing harm is not love-it is negligence.

Boundaries after childbirth

Celia told *Ugonma* her friend about a man named *Daniel* who was interested in her. They later married. *Celia* was pregnant and needed a cesarean section during childbirth to ensure her safety and that of the baby due to complications. She gave birth to a healthy baby boy and stayed at the hospital for few days. Four days after returning home, her husband asked for intimacy. *Celia* said no that she just came back from the hospital with a cesarean and that the wound was still fresh. *Daniel* insisted and Celia gave in. *Daniel's* mother, who had come to assist *Celia*, observed her coming out from *Daniel's* room. She expressed displeasure, emphasizing that the wound was still fresh and asserting that *Celia's* well-being should take precedence.

What do you think *Celia* should have done?

Oh no, this is serious and concerning. A woman who has just had a C-section must not have sex after weeks even. her health and safety come first.

She should refuse intimacy immediately

- A C-section is major abdominal surgery.
- Doctors usually advise no sex for at least 6 weeks (sometimes longer).

Sex this early can cause:

- Severe infection
- Internal bleeding
- Wound reopening

- Life-threatening complications
- She is not being difficult but rather she is protecting her life.
- She should obey her doctor, not her husband's demands.
- If possible, she should ask the doctor or nurse to explain this directly to the husband, so it's clear this is medical not personal.

Understand that this is not normal or acceptable

A husband who demands sex days after surgery ignores medical risk and prioritizes intimacy over healing. He is showing lack of care, empathy, and responsibility.

Note: Marriage does not remove a woman's right to say no. She should protect herself physically:

- Avoid lifting, stress, or pressure.
- Focus on wound care, rest and breast-feeding recovery.
- Watch for signs of infection (fever, pain, discharge) and return to hospital if needed.
- Seek by telling a trusted friend (family member, elder, pastor, counselor or healthcare worker).
- If she feels pressure or unsafe, this is reproductive coercion and marital abuse—she deserves help.

Note: A man who loves his wife protects her healing, not endangers it. Common problems arising in marriages could include:

- Communication breakdown: Issues are swept under the rug, creating an "elephant in the room".
- Emotional Distance: Partners feel alone, misunderstood, and unloved within the marriage.
- Lack of appreciation: Sacrifices like the wife's illness go unnoticed, leading to resentment.
- Betrayal and Infidelity: Emotional or physical affairs destroy trust.

- Focus on the wrong things: Chasing material wealth or external success over intimate connection.

These stories serve as poignant, appreciation and seeing beyond the surface, as highlighted in this article from Gauraw.com.

Infidelity and aftermath

- Listen, *Ulokanjo* had a misunderstanding with his wife *Chinyere* that gives birth without control. Six children in five years. He ran away from the house saying that if *Chinyere* finds out about his infidelity that she would kill him. During this time, *Chinyere* remained unaware of the reasons for her husband's absence. She contacted *Ulokanjo* by mobile phone on a designated day, but he informed her that he did not intend to return home. When Chinyere inquired about his decision, he replied that he preferred divorce over continuing their marriage. Distressed, *Chinyere* appealed to him earnestly, expressing forgiveness and requesting his return.

Person	Event	Action	Reason	Response
Ulokanjo	Misunderstanding with Chinyere	Ran away from house	Ulokanjo has been cheating on Chinyere, his beloved wife	Preferred divorce over continuing marriage
Chinyere	Ulokanjo absent	Contacted Ulokanjo by mobile phone	Unaware of reasons for absence	Appealed earnestly, expressed forgiveness, requested return

What is the way forward for Chinyere?

When a husband leaves due to infidelity and refuses to return despite his wife's pleas, the wife should focus on self and the children, self-care, seeking professional help (individual, family or friends and couples therapy). Understanding the root causes (not just justifying his actions), respecting his need for space (if he is overwhelmed) and preparing for potential outcomes (reconciliation or separation), emphasizing accountability and genuine remorse from him if healing is possible, not just begging.

His perspective: He needs to see and understand the pain his infidelity caused her, but she also needs to understand his reasons for leaving (not as justification, but for clarity).

Healing takes time; there is no quick fix.

Chinyere needs to protect herself legally and financially. Words have serious repercussions/consequences.

Ibiene became depressed when her husband, Iyowuna, spoke to her without realizing they had both just returned home from work together. She quickly went to the kitchen to make food, while her husband sat in the living room reading the newspaper and watching TV. While Ibiene stepped out with soup on the stove, Iyowuna asked if the food was ready; she replied it wasn't. The husband, upset. His response came sharp and unexpected, he said:

"Don't worry, soon I'll be a millionaire, and you won't share in my wealth."

The words struck deeply. Surprised, Ibiene replied that after 11 years together and three children, she deserved more respect. Ibiene expected partnership and respect, not contempt. She did not grasp the seriousness of his words or realize her husband's intentions. She brushed the comment aside, telling herself it was only anger speaking. She did not realize she had just heard the truth disguised as a threat.

Two years later, when money began to come, Iyowuna changed. He started infidelity, and went out of the family house where he was living with Ibiene and the children. He caused problems and left as he had threatened. Ibiene pleaded with him to return, but he refused.

What advice would you give to Ibiene?

- ***Accept that words reveal intentions:***

Iyowuna's statement was not just anger—it revealed pride, emotional distance, and a power mindset. Ibiene should stop minimizing what was said and recognize it as a warning sign.

- ***Let go of self-blame.***

She did nothing wrong by asking for respect after 11 years and three children Wanting dignity in marriage is not demanding too much.

- ***Stop pleading for someone who has chosen to leave.***

Since he left as he had threatened to and refused to return, continued pleading only deepens her pain. She cannot force accountability or love from someone unwilling to give it.

- ***Focus on emotional and financial stability.***

Ibiene should prioritize herself and her children—seek work, skills, or support systems that make her independent and secure.

- ***Seek counseling or trusted guidance.***

Speaking with a counselor, faith leader, or mature mentor can help her heal, rebuild confidence, and make wise long-term decisions.

- ***Protect her dignity and boundaries.***

If reconciliation is ever considered, it must come with humility, accountability, and change behavior—not promises or money.

- ***Teach her children by example.***

By choosing self-respect, she models strength, resilience, and healthy boundaries for her children.

In summary:

Ibiene should grieve the loss, learn from the experience, rebuild her life with courage, and never allow words—or wealth—to strip her of her worth.

LIFE LESSONS

When someone shows you who they are, listen early.

Respect is not optional in love, and silence in the face of disrespect only delays healing. Words spoken in anger often reveal hidden intentions.

Love without respect is a warning, not a phase.

Never ignore repeated signs of emotional neglect or pride. Self-worth must not be tied to a partner's promises or wealth. Strength begins when you choose dignity over desperation.

Check well, do not marry your enemy. Wolf in sheep clothing.

Tamuno, a young and promising man, had a friend named Chidubem who was known for being indiscriminate in his relationships with women regardless of their status or background, which made him a negative influence on Tamuno. Chidubem was married with children. One afternoon at around 1:00 p.m., Tamuno met Adaugo, a nurse, as she was heading to work. They greeted each other, and about six months later, they met again. During this meeting, Tamuno proposed, expressing his love and desire to marry her. Adaugo considered the proposal and told Tamuno she would inform her parents. Adaugo was concentrating on the present and not thinking about their future togetherness.

Following Igbo tradition, Adaugo's parents requested that she bring Tamuno to meet them. After meeting him, her parents decided they did not want him for their daughter, though they didn't state their objection directly. Nevertheless, Tamuno and Adaugo began dating. Her parents disapproved of the relationship, and noticing their feelings, Adaugo asked them to accept Tamuno, emphasizing his kindness, compassion, and education.

In the meantime, Adaugo dreamed that she should not marry Tamuno, foreseeing that he would eventually divorce her and pursue another woman because of his uncontrollable anger and hidden infidelity.

After eleven years, Adaugo and her family traveled to another country. While at the beach, Tamuno shocked Adaugo by telling her that they would not be living together. Concerned about their young children, Adaugo asked if it would be better for their family to stay together. Tamuno's angry response left Adaugo in tears, regretting her decision to marry him. He insisted that she return to their home country to care for his elderly father, arguing that it would be too difficult for the children to learn a new language at their age—offering what seemed like weak excuses. Tamuno ultimately chose divorce over staying with Adaugo and the kids.

Adaugo confided in her friend Erinma, who was surprised and advised her to focus on herself and her children instead of crying. Erinma speculated about Tamuno's motives, suggesting he might be seeing other women, which made Adaugo uncomfortable; she maintained her trust in her husband, believing he loved her and would never cheat. However, during an intimate moment, Tamuno accidentally called out another woman's name. When confronted, he simply apologized, and that was when Adaugo realized something was truly wrong in their relationship.

What guidance will you offer Adaugo?

Adaugo's situation involves more than simple misunderstandings; it reveals recurring warning signals that endanger her security, self-respect, and prospects. Any advice provided should be direct, decisive, and focused on her well-being.

Take warning signs seriously—before and after marriage

Anger, secrecy, infidelity, emotional manipulation, and avoiding responsibility tend to worsen over time. Love should be clear and honest, not hidden or confusing. Issues ignored before marriage often grow after.

1. Trust consistent actions, not words or apologies: Tamuno's behavior—refusing to live together, choosing divorce over family unity, calling another woman's name during intimacy—shows divided loyalty.
2. Apology without change is not repentance; they are delays.
3. Prioritize your emotional health and your children's well-being: A marriage that constantly brings fear, tears, and insecurity damages not only you but also your children. Children need stability, peace, and a present parent more than they need the image of an intact marriage.
4. Do not stay in a marriage out of fear, pressure or hope of change: Marriage should be a partnership, not a burden you carry alone. Staying with someone who has already emotionally exited/left the marriage only prolongs pain.
5. Seek wise counsel—not just friendly sympathy: Speak with trusted elders, counselors, or spiritual leaders who will tell you the truth, not just comfort you. Good counsel protects your future, not just your feelings.
6. Rebuild your identity beyond marriage. You are more than a wife someone neglects. Focus on your worth, independence, healing and purpose. A healthy marriage complements a whole person; it does not define her value.
7. For future marriage decisions: observe character, not charm. Before marriage, look for: Emotional maturity, Accountability, Respect for women, Ability to handle anger, Faithfulness in small things, Willingness to take necessary, Charm fades: character remains.

CORE LESSON

Do not marry or remain married to someone who consistently shows you that they do not value unity, honesty, and commitment. Peace of mind is not selfish: it is necessary.

Adaugo's story teaches a difficult but necessary truth: love that harms, confuses, or abandons responsibility does not love to be endured—it is a warning to be heeded.

Peace is a requirement, not a luxury. Actions speak louder than promises.

Ultimately, this story shows that self-worth should not be compromised for marriage. Marriage requires mutual respect and shared goals; leaving an emotionally harmful relationship is an act of wisdom, not failure.

EPILOGUE

All through ages, the family remains both central and strong. For centuries it has withstood social catastrophes and revolutions—but it has remained unchanged by them. We are at a crossroads between what the family has been, and what it will become in the future. Childhood, parenthood, and old age are all likely to be redefined. The emergence of a new political class of older people, for example, is just one issue families and governments still have to grapple with. As human society becomes more complex, the great diversity of family lives and forms is expected to continue.

It is necessary for us to invest in families, if not we may pay a high price. For most individuals, the family is by far the most significant institution. Whether we grow up anxious or confident, trusting or suspicious, ambitious or content is determined very largely by our early experiences of family life. Evils which a well-supported family and childhood can reduce or eliminate are as follows: addiction, ill health, crime, school drop-out rates and callous self-interest. Measures to tackle serious family crises—abandonment, abuse and neglect, and marital breakdown—are essential in all societies.

Protecting and empowering the family is of crucial importance if those future generations are to enjoy a decent quality of life. The family is the most fundamental resource for human society. Guaranteeing the transfer of resources between generations is fundamental to the notion of 'sustainability'. The present generation has a responsibility to future ones to provide a healthier, more secure environment for the family to act out its role in human society. Family is the fundamental bed rock of human beings.

BIBLIOGRAPHY

1. Boyden, J. Families (celebrate and hope in a world of change)
   Gala Books Ltd, 66 Charlotte Street, London
   WIPIR, 1993.
2. United Nations,
   Living Arrangements of "Women and Their Children in Developing Countries United Nations."
   Publication Sales No. E.96X11.5, 1995
3. Maria, M.
   Violence Against Women. A United Nations Publication.
   Campaign for Women's Human Rights,
   A Life Free of Violence
4. Basu, Alaka.
   Relationship of Women's Economic Roles to Child
   Health and Well-being. Paper prepared for the United
   Nations experts group meeting on population and women,
   Gaborone, Botswana, 22-26 June, 1992
5. Bruce, Judith and Cynthia, B Lloyd (1992).
   Beyond female headship: Family research and policy issues for the 1990s. Paper presented at the workshop on Research. Methods 12-14 February, 1992. Washington. Finding the ties that bind beyond leadership and household. Working paper No.41. New York .The Population Council.
6. Ono-osaki, Keiko, (1991).

Female headed household in developing countries: By choice or by circumstances. In demographic and health surveys world conference proceedings, Vol.111. Columbia Maryland: Institute for Resource Development/Macro Systems, Inc., pp. 1603-1622.

7. Violence against Women:
(Paulines Publications Africa Daughters of St Paul
ISBN 9966-21- 321-X. 1997 edition. Nairobi-Kenya.)

8. Domestic Violence: New York State Office for the Prevention of Domestic Violence. (1996, 2000, 2008, 2010).

9. Counselling Skills for Dummies - A Wiley Brand.
2nd Edition by Gail Evans. (2013)

10. George Forman, Fatherhood (2008).

11. Poverty and Homelessness, Mary, E. Williams. (2004).

12. Inner-City Poverty, Tamara L. Roleff (2003)

13. George Forman, Fatherhood (2008).

14. Poverty and Homelessness, Mary, E. Williams. (2004).

15. Inner-City Poverty, Tamara L. Roleff (2003).

16. Substance Abuse Treatment and Family Therapy, Treatment Improvement Protocol TIP 39 by SAMHA, 2004.

17. The Story of Life by Marianne Taylor, Published 2020 by Unipress Books Ltd.

18. Natural Woman by Dr. Leslie Korn, 2020 published by Shambhala publications, Inc.

19. Divorce and Money - Make The Best Financial Decisions During Divorce 13th Edition by Attorneys Violet Woodhouse CFLS, Lina Guillen 2000-2019.

20. The Secret that will Revolutionize Your Relationship – The 5 Love Languages by Gary Chapman, 2017.

21. Contemplating Divorce by Susan Peace Gadoua, LCSW 2008.

22. John M. Gottman, PH. D, Julie Schwartz Gottman, PHD and Joan Declaire
Ten Lessons to Transform Our Marriage - Seven Principles for Making Marriage Work 2006.

23. A Hopeful Approach to Saving Relationships - This is How Your Marriage Ends by Matthew Fray, 2022.

THE STORM IN MY MARRIAGE: THE STORY BEHIND 'FAMILY STORM'

A Journey Through Turbulence, Transformation, and Triumph

Introduction

Every marriage, like the shifting tides of the ocean, encounters its own tempests—moments where currents of conflict, pain, and uncertainty surge. For me, those stormy years were not just a test of commitment, but the crucible in which my book, Family Storm, was conceived. This is the biography of that storm: the struggle, the heartbreak, the lessons, and the healing that ultimately inspired me to write the story of my family's most turbulent chapter.

Early Days: The Calm Before the Storm

Our marriage, like so many others, began in the warm glow of hope and promise. We built our life together on shared dreams: a home filled with laughter, children filling the rooms with innocent chaos, and the comfort of knowing we were each other's anchor.

For years, we weathered minor squalls—differences about finances, parenting, and the usual ebb and flow of intimacy. Yet, there was always a sense of equilibrium, a belief that love was enough to keep us afloat. But beneath the calm surface, subtle undercurrents of resentment and unmet expectations began to swirl.

A Couple Involved in Infidelity

This may create problems at home, particularly by ignoring the children's needs. Bringing a new person into the family may create changes in established relationships. Being unfaithful to your spouse can damage trust in the relationship. Additionally, involving someone else may lead to complications and unintended consequences.

The Gathering Clouds: Signs of Trouble

It is easy to overlook the first warning signs—a missed date night, a harsh word left unaddressed, the growing silence at the dinner table. Slowly, small disputes became recurring arguments, and the gulf between us widened.

We both changed: work pressures mounted, dreams were deferred, and communication, once our lifeline, grew brittle and frayed. I found myself oscillating between anger and sorrow, at times feeling isolated even with the children around.

The Eye of the Storm: Betrayal and Loss

The storm broke in earnest when trust was shattered. I discovered secrets—hidden messages, unexplained absences—that hinted at emotional betrayals. Pain crashed into our home with the force of a hurricane, toppling the fragile structures of trust we had built.

Grief is a strange companion. It dulls reason, amplifies insecurities, and at its worst, erodes the sense of self. For months, every conversation felt like walking on broken glass. Our children sensed the tension, their joyful laughter giving way to guarded glances and quiet questions.

Surviving the Tempest: Seeking Help and Clarity

It became clear that we could not navigate these waters alone. We sought counseling, not just as a desperate measure, but as a lifeline thrown into the churning sea of our relationship. Parents could not settle the problem due to the wrong approach.

There were nights spent apart, and days when the weight of resentment felt too heavy to carry. Yet, amid the chaos, a quiet determination grew within me: if we were to survive this storm, I needed to rediscover my own voice and purpose.

Journaling Through the Rain

Friends and relatives inspired me to start writing. I began to write—first in fragments, just scribbled notes capturing my anger, sadness, and hope. My journal became a hidden attic, storing memories that were too heavy to keep in the open. I wrote about sleepless nights, about the moments of unexpected tenderness that survived even the darkest days, and about the questions I feared asking out loud.

Soon, my entries became stories, and the stories began to form the skeleton of a book. Writing offered me clarity—a way to make sense of what felt senseless, a means to find beauty in the pain.

The Turning Point: Forgiveness and Healing

Healing does not arrive like a gentle rain; it comes in fits and starts, punctuated by setbacks and revelations. Over time, I learned to forgive. Forgiveness is a sweet thing. It is for your emotional, physical, social and psychological wellness.

Marriage, I realized, is not the absence of storms, but the willingness to rebuild together after the clouds have passed. Our children, resilient and wise beyond their years, taught me the power of grace. They reminded us, sometimes wordlessly, that love—even battered and bruised—could be a lesson learned to shape you better.

The Birth of 'Family Storm'

As the intensity of the tempest faded, my journal entries transformed into chapters. I wanted to tell the truth, to strip away the facade of perfect families and reveal the raw, complicated reality of love and commitment. Family Storm is not just a memoir; it is a testament to the resilience of ordinary people faced with extraordinary challenges.

Writing the book was an act of catharsis and courage. I shared not only my pain, but also the moments of hope and the lessons we learned:

- That vulnerability is a source of strength.
- That forgiveness is not a single act, but an ongoing process.

Life After the Storm

Family Storm has touched readers who see themselves in its pages. People have written to share their own stories of pain and reconciliation, of heartbreak and hope. The book has become a lighthouse for those navigating their own tempests, a reminder that they are not alone.

To anyone standing in the eye of their own family storm, I offer this: The winds will abate, the rain will cease, and with courage, you can chart a new course. May the story of my storm, and the hope embedded in Family Storm, be a lantern for you in the darkness testament to the power of surviving, and thriving, after the worst has passed.

ABOUT THE AUTHOR

Dame Beatrice Ndudim Goldson-Nwalozie holds a BEd in Education/Biology from the University of Port Harcourt and an MEd in Guidance and Counseling from Abia State University, Nigeria. She has extensive high school teaching experience and enjoys writing, mentoring, tutoring, and counseling. Beatrice lives in the United States of America, working in different organizations in New York City. Beatrice works as a Substance Use Specialist with the Services for the Underserved (S:US) ACT team. As a certified Alcohol and Substance Abuse Counselor (CASAC), she views addiction as a disease and believes in the possibility of recovery. Her books have served as research references for college students and supported many families.

Beatrice published her first book, **Family Drama**, in 2017 with Trafford publishers. The second edition, subtitled **Attractive Parcel**, was released by Toplink publishers, while her latest, **Family Storm: Surviving the Turbulence**, came out from ARPress in 2026. She is currently working on **Den of Love: Ringing Hope**.

Beatrice has three children, one daughter and two sons—and is also a grandmother. She was previously married for 12 years; she is now a single parent. She has a large extended family with several siblings, aunties, and uncles.

She is radiant, independent, cheerful, friendly, and generous. In her free time, she enjoys singing, watching soccer, and visiting the sick to provide support and gifts.